Lauren was fantastic. She patterned everything to us, rather than us having to change to a realtor's style. She found out our needs and fit our timetable. She gave us very good insight around what we needed to do get the house ready to sell. She was very thorough on inspecting the house and seeing what needs to be done. She far exceeded our expectations.
–Kat

I liked the fact that Lauren was just a seller's agent. I didn't know those existed. That made a huge difference because she wasn't out there showing other people houses. She was focused on this house. It was about us, and not just the commission and sales process. I felt like she was working for us. My mom had lived in that house for 45 years. She made my mom feel comfortable. She was always there. When my sisters in Texas called, Lauren would get right back to them. She'd explain things in a way they understood. Even after the house sold, we'd call her with questions and she would answer them. She has an amazing photographer that comes in and takes pictures. She does so much stuff up front, the house sells itself.
–Karolyn Bryant

Lauren was extremely professional and approachable. Lauren was very honest about improvements we needed to do in order to sell our condo. She had great references to help. Lauren was very friendly and communicated very well. She is a very good negotiator who explained everything in a manner that we could fully understand. Very trustworthy and highly recommended. I have had loved ones who have experienced quite the difference in their home buying/selling and only wish she could have done the job.
– Jennifer & Eddie Matte

Lauren was phenomenal. She knows what she's doing. She took charge. She explained all the legal parts of the process and how she would move forward if we listed with her. I was impressed with her all the way through. She knew what she was talking about. She helped me list it at a good price. We ended up selling within a few days and made a nice profit. With Lauren, you can be confident you're in good hands.
– Kevin Gladden

Lauren is straight-forward and direct. She's very dedicated. She makes sure all the i's are dotted and the t's are crossed, which is a big deal with contracts because you want to make sure they are done right. She's also good at negotiating prices. She really stands up for you and represents your best interests. She's good at identifying what might make a property work or thinking outside the box.
– Becky Thomas

I had another realtor before Lauren, and the house didn't sell for more than a year. When that contract was over, I hired Lauren. And it sold like that. I had it listed at a price, and Lauren got it sold for $2,000 over that price. It didn't even take a month. She sold the place right away.
– Happy Seller

We worked with a couple of realtors before I contacted Lauren, and she was the best realtor to work with. It was like working with a friend. She understood what we wanted. She did a great job. She explained everything to the smallest detail. She'll take the time to negotiate the price for you and to do the research. She's knows the market.
– Zeyad Ameen

Working with Lauren is like working with a friend. She does what she says she's going to do. Her knowledge of the market was very beneficial to me. Lauren told me what I needed to do to put my house on the market. It was very minimal. Another realtor wanted me to spend $20,000. The property I sold with her wasn't in the best shape, but she got me what I wanted as far as price was concerned. I called Lauren one day and two days later it sold.
– BJ Lewis

We'd heard a lot of horror stories. We were dreading the process. But it was so much easier than what we were expecting and I credit Lauren with most of that. I really appreciated the time she spent with us. She put our needs over her own. Lauren really knows what she's talking about. She really goes the extra mile.
– Rachel Bachmann

When we decided to work with Lauren, she had a bundle of information and walked us through every step of every phase. We had heard all the horror stories, but after she walked us through it, it wasn't daunting anymore. She's very thorough in making sure you understand the next step in the process. She never made us feel like we were asking too many questions.
– Dave Burgess

I bought a house several years ago, and it was the worst experience. I told my lender what had happened and she gave me Lauren's name. She is the absolute best! One of the things I said to Lauren was, "Keep me in the loop." And she did. I was so impressed with her. She's alert to little things that can happen, and when they do, she's ready. She's very, very smart.
– Kathleen Cramer

Lauren was phenomenal to work with. I felt like she was a partner. I felt like she was a friend helping me sell my house, rather than a professional I just hired in to do a job. She is proactive, helpful, and thoughtful. She would give us things to work on. She wouldn't hold back or sugar coat things just because we didn't want to hear it. As sellers, you're very tied to your home. You have a lot of emotion invested in it. Sometimes it can be difficult to hear there are things you need to improve or change before you leave. It was really helpful to have that list of items – what we can work on now, what we need to think about, and what we don't need to pay attention to. It helped us feel more prepared to sell our house. Lauren made the process seamless. She told us exactly what to expect and gave us very realistic timelines. She helped us with the deadlines and set reasonable expectations all throughout the process. I felt really prepared. It sold within two weeks. She did a really great job marketing our home. She put it in front of the right audiences. She took a lot of time to get quality photos of our house. You look at the photos and you think, "This is a nice home. I want to live here!" She was very good at communicating, checking in, seeing how we were doing, asking us if we had any questions. She was incredibly knowledgeable about her job, very smart about the market, and very strategic about her marketing and how she was going to tell our house's story. I think it's helpful that Lauren is really involved in the community. She knows how to target her marketing. She knows what will be key selling points in the description. She understands the buyers and the sellers. I would recommend Lauren in a heartbeat.

– Alyssa Parker

Working with Lauren was fabulous. She was always very attentive. She went the extra mile to answer all our questions, and she did extra work another realtor might not do. We appreciated her entire demeanor … the way she handled the entire process. She made it very easy for us, answering questions all along the way.
– Ben Martin

Lauren was very professional. I didn't have any surprises or gotchas working with her. She was very patient explaining things. She explained clearly. She gave me information about the process that I wasn't aware of. If you need someone who is a go-getter, who is smart, knows the process, and will hold your hand through it, Lauren is the one!
– Sharon Simpson-Dogon

Lauren is awesome. She mimicked my sense of urgency, but not in a pushy way. She's really smart, was realistic about how my house would sell, and gave good advice about what to fix or not fix. She had a great photographer. She put together a video to show the house. The technology she used for scheduling showings was really cool, and sending documents via e-mail that I could sign and send back on my phone made things really easy. My house was only on the market for 5 days and I had a full offer.
– E. Murphy

Working with Lauren was wonderful. She was extremely knowledgeable and professional. I appreciated her attention to detail. She gave great advice! We actually ended up with a bidding war. I never felt like I had to call her to follow up. She was on top of everything. She never left me hanging. I will definitely refer her to others.
– Cheryl Westendorf

Lauren is results-oriented and focused. She's friendly, but also no-nonsense. She doesn't procrastinate, and she doesn't make excuses. I have worked with quite a few terrific realtors, and even among them, Lauren stands out as a star. Lauren went above and beyond to help me sell my home.
– Mary Lynne Ashley

I loved what Lauren did with my listing. I loved the photos she took ... how she showed the property and the whole community. I was impressed with how she presented the property online. I love looking at Realtor.com and a lot of the photos are really bad. But Lauren knew the best ways to market my property. She gave me great advice. She gave really good opinions about how to present the property and how to price it. She always took my calls. She stayed in communication with me. I don't think another realtor would have gotten it sold that fast and at that price. I had a goal and she helped me achieve it. She was everything I hoped for in a realtor and more.
– Donna Sohan

We had a really fantastic experience working with Lauren. She was always very energetic and positive, and she got us a great price for our house. When she first told us the price she planned to ask for the house, I thought she was crazy. [It was $20,000 more than what any house in our neighborhood had EVER sold for.] I went with it because she was the professional and she knew the market. We ended up selling for $12,000 over the asking price! The marketing she did for the house was top notch. She always kept us informed about what was going on. My previous experience with a realtor wasn't a good one, so I was a little skeptical. He was pushy and couldn't understand what I wanted. But with Lauren it was an amazingly positive experience.
– David

Lauren makes everything super easy. It can be stressful selling a house – that much money. It's extremely important to have someone qualified to help you out in taking a huge step forward in your life. I talked to a couple of other realtors before Lauren. I'm very picky when working with people. I want them to be competent and intelligent and ready to work. Lauren's experience was noticeable. I trusted her. I had multiple offers so I could choose who to sell it to. I definitely made a profit off of it. I was in Texas most of the time I was selling my condo in Colorado. Lauren pretty much handled everything I couldn't do. The condo had people living in it – it was being rented out – so she was able to find someone to clean it out. She found someone to make necessary repairs. She went above and beyond.

– D. Arellano

Lauren was able to get us an appraisal higher than any other realtor. She does it based on your house – how individual it is when compared to all the others. You can have a similar house right next to you, but if you put $50,000 worth of stuff inside, Lauren makes sure the appraiser recognizes that. We interviewed five realtors, and all the other realtors said, "This is what has been selling in your neighborhood. You're not going to get over this amount." Lauren was able to get about $64,000 more than any other realtor. The pictures she took and the layout she did was unbelievable. It was better than any we saw on the internet for selling other people's homes. It was amazing. Lauren also had a link where you could go in and see statistics – how many people looked at your house and what their comments were. That link was really, really good. She's very, very thorough.

– Sheila and Mike

The Psychological Secrets That Sell Your Property for More

HOW TO MAKE AN EXTRA $40,000 OF PROFIT BY THINKING LIKE A SHARK TANK INVESTOR

Lauren Collier

www.LiveDreamColorado.com

Published in Colorado Springs, Colorado

The Psychological Secrets That Sell Your Property for More/ Lauren Collier —1st ed.
ISBN 978-1-948415-00-2

First Edition

Never would I have lived up to my dream of writing this book without the support of my business partner Rob and his family and my beloved Robert. I'm grateful to those who have come into my life and chosen to stay, and made me a better person for it. Thank you for your insight and your support, for your encouragement and your faith. Your confidence in me has bridged the gap when I needed it most, and it's meant the world to me. And finally, to Fiona, the best dog in the world. She taught me how to love - if I can bring a small portion of the light, happiness and love into the world that she brought to me, then her bright and caring spirit will continue to live on.

-Lauren

Contents

DISCLAIMER

This book is not endorsed by or associated with *Shark Tank TV* or the Shark Tank investors. The content of this book is based on study, research, and application of the strategies publicly used on Shark Tank. All views and opinions in this book belong to the author and are not representative of *Shark Tank*, the Shark Tank investors, or their associated companies.

Foreword

"How did you go from law to marketing?"

I'm often asked this question. My eclectic professional background confuses people. I'm the founder and principal of HugSpeak, a communication strategy firm focusing heavily on custom market research and effective use of digital media — but I also have two law degrees and spent years as a trial attorney.

To me, the connection is obvious. Law is about persuading people – judges, juries, opposing counsel. Marketing is about persuading people too – customers, constituents, donors, decision-makers, buyers. I use the same basic persuasion techniques in the courtroom as I do when crafting a digital strategy for a corporation, a non-profit, or a small business.

And that's why I love this book!

No. Really. I *love* this book!

Because just like law or marketing, selling a home for the highest possible price requires effective persuasion techniques and expert marketing know-how – something Lauren Collier, the author, understands more than any other real estate professional I've ever met. We may not always use the same terminology – she says "selling secrets" and I say "persuasion techniques"—but we're talking about the same thing. We both help people achieve a desired outcome by understanding their audience and presenting their case, their product, their company, or their home in a way that appeals to that audience.

By tapping into "sales pitch" lessons from the wildly popular television show *Shark Tank* and using examples from her years of experience as a highly successful real estate professional, Lauren has created a comprehensive yet easy-to-follow guide for selling your home at the maximum price possible. While the secrets she shares are geared toward people looking to sell a house, they are solid principals for all sales, marketing, and persuasion – presented in a concise and conversational manner. This book is a quick and breezy read, but it is chock full of actionable tips, strategies, and insights. Readers who heed Lauren's sound and well-founded advice will undoubtedly make more from the sale of their home than they thought possible.

As a real estate professional, Lauren cares deeply about providing the absolute best information, customer service, and overall experience to her clients as possible. Not only have I witnessed her professionalism, expertise, friendliness, and impressive sales results first-hand, my company has also conducted her customer satisfaction studies for the past six years. I've done a lot of customer research in my career, and I can honestly say I have *never* seen such consistent, glowing responses as the ones Lauren receives. Year after year, her clients RAVE about her! And they frequently report delight at the price they received for their home after following Lauren's "selling secrets".

As an author, Lauren demonstrates that same level of care for her readers. She truly wants all home sellers to have a positive selling experience. That's why you'll find chapters like *Why don't all real estate agents share these* secrets?, *Dangerous Dynamics and How to Protect Yourself*, *Talk is Cheap*, and *Behind the Scenes* devoted to explaining how most real estate agents think, what motivates them, why they might not have your best interests at heart, how to evaluate agents, and how to find the right agent for you.

In addition to explaining how the real estate profession works – and how that impacts sellers like you – Lauren walks you step by step through properly valuing your home (*Know Your Product*), presenting your home in a way that makes a great impression on the right buyers (*You Never Get a Second Chance*), and generating or tapping into demand for your home (*Everybody Wants to Have*). Every chapter is carefully crafted to provide you with expert insight, clear examples, inspiring stories, and specific tactics to maximize your profit. Every page reveals Lauren's passion for empowering sellers.

Lauren wants you to be a winner in the real estate market. If you want to make the most money possible on the sale of your home, **read this book!** In fact, anyone wanting to learn more about sales secrets or persuasion techniques will find this book well worth their attention. You can trust me on that. I'm a persuasion expert.

Lauren M. Hug, J.D., LL.M.
Principal and Founder of HugSpeak

Why don't all real estate agents share these secrets?

A ny real estate agent you hire will maximize your sale profit...won't they? Unfortunately no, for many reasons we'll discuss throughout this book.

Many got licensed to sell real estate because they didn't know what else to do. That's a terrible reason if you ask me, but it's often-cited nonetheless. They didn't attend years of specialized school like doctors, lawyers, engineers, or anyone else you'd entrust to handle transactions worth hundreds of thousands of dollars.

Having completed a terrifyingly short training (two weeks' classroom time in Colorado!), too many licensed agents know the bare minimum - nothing more than how to answer a few multiple choice questions on the entry exam. Not one of those questions is about how to attract the highest offers for your property. For passing the exam and receiving a license to sell real estate, knowing how sell property for maximum price is absolutely unnecessary.

Most agents haven't studied psychological marketing, nor economics. They aren't experts in preparing properties to sell for the highest profit, developing effective price strategies, or negotiating for the seller. Ignorance about how to maximize return on investment prevails in the industry, despite the public's perception that real estate agents are specialists in this matter.

They just flip through a standard listing presentation provided by their brokerage, convincing not only the unwitting sellers but also themselves that they're best for the job. Having never learned how to get maximize your return on investment, they don't add value to your transaction. Worse yet, they don't know what they don't know.

On the other hand, having an expert on your side implementing specific strategies to raise your profit can make all the difference. That's why I've compiled this information – to improve seller success.

Another reason many agents don't share this information – secrets that can net you $40,000 or more extra profit on your home sale - is their "Faster is Better" mentality. It is *rampant*! No matter that strategic property preparation can yield you a lot of extra money, many real estate agents ain't got time for that. They put pressure on you to list the property immediately with them.

If they took their time, tailoring marketing to the specific property and owner circumstance, negotiating for the best price and terms, and treating every client like they'd treat their best friend, they couldn't sign as many contracts. They'd never win the High Volume award at their firm (more about that in Chapter 7).

I'm sorry to say this, but it's a real fact. Real estate sales *is* a commission-driven industry where the salesperson's income relies *only* on the number of properties they sell. So the faster they can secure *your* signature to list with them, the faster they can move on to the next owner and rush them to sign a contract too.

For this type of agent, time on expert consultation, property preparation, and high-yielding magnetic marketing is a total waste. As long as you sell with *them*, that's all that matters. How much profit *you* make - - or lose - - at closing is of absolutely no concern at all to them.

Agent manipulativeness and ego are complicit in keeping the Selling Secrets out of property owners' hands too.

A key tenet of many well-known agent sales training programs is to purposely confuse, evade, and intimidate the property owner. (I feel sick writing that sentence...but the truth should be known.) The programs teach that to get hired to list a property, the agent need not train for superior industry knowledge, marketing expertise, or even negotiating ability, but only for the ability (and willingness) to deliver the highest-converting sales ploy. Ploys are sales tactics designed to convince property sellers to list with that agent immediately.

Their "better than you" attitude is a strategy they use to sign listings. They need you to believe that they have special powers, and maintaining this image requires them to keep *you* in the dark about profitable selling strategies.

I'll tell you, I love my job and the wonderful feeling of negotiating successful property sales for people. It's important and rewarding work. There's a lot to learn in order to achieve the kind of results we get for our clients. But, I want to *share* information with my clients to maximize the result of their home sale, not hide it! That's why I wrote this book.

Finally, there are agents who just don't care about helping people. They've been in business too long and simply aren't concerned about quality anymore, if they ever were. They don't embrace technological advances, so what they can offer is very limited. They're in a hurry, not because they have more sales to make, but because they have "more important things to do" like play golf, drink with buddies, and vacation. They just don't care that their attitude hurts you and your bottom line. They don't lose a wink of sleep over it. If you could have made more money, "oh well." To them, your profit or loss is just not their problem. Like a lazy employee anywhere, they'll do the minimum and if you don't like it you can "hire someone else".

But here's the thing – few property owners are familiar with how to spot a lazy agent. When you don't know what to look for, you run the risk of losing money. When an agent who doesn't care lists your property, you will sell for less than you should have. Watch for the warning signs and get someone on your side who's knowledgeable, committed, and dedicated to earning you maximum return on your property investment.

I'm sick of seeing sellers become victims of real estate agents who intentionally keep them shrouded in the dark. I'm tired of hearing about agents who take advantage of people! The misdeeds of certain players in this industry some days seem like they have no end. I can't stand to see good people taken advantage of. If it were up to me, it would all come to a halt right here.

My next book may be a collection of real estate horror stories. If you have one, send it my way so I can include it. I've heard so many already, but each still shocks me more than the last.

This book is my first step to stop the pushiness, carelessness, egotistism, manipulativeness, and unprofessionalism. And to usher in a new era of property sellers demanding that *their* needs come first. You deserve quality service and expert advice that will produce the most profitable sale for you.

Researching these Psychological Secrets That Sell Your Property for More and developing an implementation plan for them has taken a lot of time. But it was the right thing to do. There *is* a better way to list and sell property, putting anywhere from a few thousand dollars to many tens of thousands of dollars of extra profit into the pockets of sellers.

I'm not interested in keeping secrets – I want to facilitate real people achieving a better life. And a real estate sale is one tremendous opportunity to *vastly* improve your financial standing - **when transacted professionally**. In this book, you'll learn how to protect yourself against bad players and how to avoid losing profit in your home sale.

CHAPTER ONE

Dangerous Dynamics and How to Protect Yourself

A troublesome trifecta costs property sellers thousands - How can you protect yourself?

Jack in the Box restaurants once ran a special called the Monster burger. It was a huge hit, and demand was overwhelming. But with employees in a rush, many burgers weren't fully cooked. As a result, four people died and 178 more were permanently injured.

All told, 732 people were infected with *E. coli* - seven hundred thirty two victims of restaurant workers who were overwhelmed and in a hurry. The 1993 Jack in the Box catastrophe quickly became the most infamous contemporary food poison outbreak, with damages in excess of $58 million.

All because of carelessness.

Just as single employee can serve hundreds of *E. coli*-infected burgers in a shift, a single agent who didn't mean any harm can cause catastrophic damage by being careless when they most needed to be careful in serving others.

I see basic errors in property listings every day. Agents fumble or completely skip the most essential elements like a full slate of eye-catching professional listing photos and an enticing, accurate property description.

Blurry, dark photos. Pictures of a toilet or a random corner of a room. Even sideways pictures. Only 1 or 5 or 8 photos instead of a full set. How will this sell the property?

Meaningless descriptions like "For sale. Has walls, roof, carpet. Enjoyable home." Or a completely missing property description. Which is worse?

Incorrect property facts like wrong house size, incorrect bathroom count, wrong school district, and inaccurate features.

Not to mention an inappropriate price. Properties are priced way too high or way too low all the time.

Carelessness of this caliber is unforgivable, yet prevalent. Errors like these lose sellers *so* much money!...Often without them even knowing it.

Just as it seems impossible that a restaurant chain as large as Jack in the Box would make a mistake as basic and devastating as serving undercooked burgers, sickening hundreds of patrons, likewise it seems impossible that an agent entrusted to sell an asset as large as a house would bungle the listing badly enough to lose the seller tens of thousands of dollars. But listings are mangled like this every day. Mistakes like inaccurate property details, missing information, and unflattering photos all *severely* undermine the seller's profit.

And don't think it's only amateur agents who do these things. Agents who list a lot of homes do these same things, to save themselves time and money – regardless of the impact on you. For any agent you interview, *carefully* check their portfolio of past listings to ensure you don't become the next victim!

According to the February 6, 1993 *New York Times* article "Jack in the Box's Worst Nightmare":

> ...the United States Agriculture Department and state health officials say the bacteria could have been killed if Jack in the Box had cooked the hamburgers at 155 degrees as required by the state, rather than at the Federal standard of 140 degrees. The company has disputed that argument and said it did not know the state increased the required cooking standard in May.

Does Jack in the Box being unaware of the new standard matter? To me, that doesn't reduce their liability whatsoever. To those who died, who were sickened, who lost friends and family members, all that matters is the devastation they endured. The restaurant *could* have saved lives with better cooking practices, but they didn't.

The very real danger of ignorance is severe. What someone in a position of trust knows or doesn't know will either help or harm innocent folks who rely on them for service.

Perhaps Jack in the Box was uninformed about new higher standards for cooking, but that doesn't let them off the hook for the damage they caused. The onus was on them to become informed and *stay* informed about safe cooking practices because they served the public in a position of trust – people had faith in them to serve food that was safe to eat. We take for granted that a restaurant will provide food we can eat without harm. Jack in the Box should have taken that level of trust very seriously – seriously enough to know the current public safety regulations and to enforce them among all workers.

Many agents, too, are woefully behind the times. If they're unaware of new standards for your protection and success, who's fault is that? Who endures the consequences?

The very low legal minimums for practicing real estate sales are much to the detriment of sellers who expect, misguidedly, that an agent will know how to perform at the highest level and will implement the most effective sale strategies available. Just like Jack in the Box, many agents don't keep up with best practices. They stick to doing the absolute minimum, which inhibits your property from selling for the highest possible profit.

Attracting the top-dollar sale price for you, using the best tools available to garner maximum profit from your investment, providing expert advice and zealous advocacy - these are expectations we rightly hold of real estate agents. The challenge is to find one who can and will execute on these expectations. Don't settle for less.

When you're ready to sell your property, avoid carelessness and ignorance. Timely, property-specific sales strategies will generate the highest return on your property investment. Implementing these requires the agent to understand effective marketing, have deep expertise in current local market conditions, and be highly attentive to your property, to extract the full profit for you.

Imagine a businessman running behind schedule for an important meeting. In a big rush, he jumps in the car and kicks it in reverse, trying to make up for lost time. He swerves in and out of traffic, speeding, doing whatever it takes to arrive on time.

Totally caught up in his own needs, he doesn't give enough attention to the most important task at hand – driving safely. He sure doesn't intend to hurt anyone, but he doesn't show an appropriate standard of care to those around him. He runs a red light and zooms through the intersection, striking another vehicle.

He injures another person and damages their car, which creates a series of burdens now *that* person has to bear, from filing an insurance claim, to waiting for car repairs, to seeking and paying for medical care. He's ruined a lot of things for the other person just because he had more important things to do that morning than pay attention to a "little thing" like a red light.

This is how a great many real estate agents operate. When a new agent joins a firm, immediately they're indoctrinated to "Sell Sell Sell". Not sell well. Just Sell and sell fast, at whatever financial shortage to the property owner. "Just get that listing contract signed," their bosses tell them, "Don't waste time consulting the seller - just get that contract signed – the faster the better!"

Sadly, I'm not joking. Customized marketing strategy? No time. Unique property details? Forget about it! They just need to Sell Sell Sell.

The faster they get a property owner to sign that listing contract, the faster they'll get paid a commission – seller's profit be damned. And they'll do this, too, at offer time, rushing you to sign an agreement to the buyer's price and terms even when a counteroffer is better for you.

Their needs trump everything. Always in a hurry, focused on their own priorities, they don't pay attention to the needs of people around them, not even the needs of the people who hired them. This type of agent will inflict both direct and collateral damage to sellers.

Sale opportunities are missed because the agent's moving too fast. They may even take advantage of their position of trust and swindle money. And in a huge number of cases, they simply short the seller on sale profit because – instead of taking time to negotiate price and terms with buyers – they rush sellers to make important decisions too quickly, so that the agent can meet their own sales numbers faster.

Why are so many agents boastful and bragging when they interview to list a property? Because they came to get what they want for themselves – your property listing and the paycheck that comes with it. Everything in between they couldn't care less about. For them, it's not about you. It's about them. They'll skip steps, give poor and incomplete advice, and high-pressure-sales you into decisions that benefit them, not you.

Some real estate agents take more transactions at once than they can handle. Plenty of others seek to work less and "take it easy" more, although they won't tell *you* that. Both types make insufficient time to fight for their clients' best interests. You sign the representation agreement with them, and they disappear. Get ready for long wait times for a call back. When problems arise, they can't be found to help. This happens *all the time*.

There are many agents who build a big reputation for themselves through TV ads, billboards, mailing campaigns, etc, and lean on "their name" to get business, not their level of service. Their ego runs the show, and sellers are expected to come along for the ride. Don't stand for that.

Even many experienced agents who *know* what's best for you often don't take the time to actually *do* what's best for you, when it conflicts with what they want for themselves.

This is how things go wrong. When the property isn't prepared for showings, when the pricing research is inaccurate and incomplete, when the marketing is riddled with errors – because the agent's time is too important to spend on those "little things" – the property *seller* becomes the victim, and the agent still gets paid. It's not fair. But it happens *all* the time.

Don't fall for a self-centered agent whose needs outweigh your own. Your property is a tremendous investment and a hugely valuable asset. You have the right to service from an agent who is competent, careful, and educated, and who takes time on your property. Make sure you enlist the help of someone who's committed to your process, your success, and your *profit* as a matter of principal, because it really *matters* to them.

Clients once shared this story with me after we closed the sale of their house. When they first invited me to their home, I was one of five agents they interviewed. After I sold their house, they told me "The sale price you got for our house was $64,000 more than the highest amount that any other agent said we could get for it."

How did this happen? How did four other agents value their house from $64,000-$100,000 lower than what we sold it for? Here's how:

Not looking closely at the details of the property and at the market conditions – Carelessness.

Not knowing how to value a unique property correctly – Ignorance.

Thinking they'd get hired no matter whether they spent time to properly research and value the home or not – Ego.

If these sellers had hired any one of the other four agents, they'd have $64,000 to $100,000 less in their bank account right now. For them, that was the difference of retiring or not. That's robbery if you ask me.

You must select an agent who has the knowledge, the time, and the dedication to prioritize you and your property sale. Don't end up a victim of carelessness, ignorance, or ego like these home sellers could have.

A real estate agent is entrusted to handle one of your most valuable assets. If they're in a hurry, disengaged, or self-absorbed, it bodes disaster for you. Moving too quickly, not investing time to hone skills, and focusing on personal interests instead of their client's needs - agent selfishness and recklessness are real dangers you want to steer clear of. Don't be the next real estate horror story. A seller cannot afford to trust the sale of their property to someone who's careless – or worst yet reckless.

You deserve better. I believe every property seller deserves attentiveness, expertise, and skill in their corner. You deserve to get ALL the profit available to you in your property sale, not just a little bit of it.

One final problem you'll want to make sure you avoid is real estate agent desperation. A real estate agent gets paid ONLY when they close a sale. There's no such thing for them as going into the office and getting a paycheck just for showing up day after day. The agent without clients, is unemployed. No income. No salary. No guarantees.

The only guarantee is that if they convince you to sign a listing contract with them (and the faster the better) and they sell your house for any price whatsoever (no matter how low) they'll get paid. That's it. No bonuses for attendance or exceptional service.

In one way it's good that the agent gets paid only when they sell your house – you're both working toward the same end goal. But the good news stops there. The problem is that many agents truly don't care how *much* they sell your house for.

Let that fact sink in.

A difference of $5,000, $20,000, or $40,000 on your property's sale price could determine what car you buy next or where you can afford to live when you move. But those same tens of thousands of dollars in profit difference for you, change the agent's pay by only a few hundred dollars.

Because the final sale price of your home affects their total pay only a tiny bit, the black-and-white objective for them – their desperate need - is to get paid *at all*. How else will they eat? How will they pay their mortgage? They must get the listing and the sale – your listing and sale – regardless of price point. Not at the highest possible sale price. Not to the seller's greatest financial gain. Not for the property owner's highest net profit. At any price whatsoever.

This fact leads desperate agents to price your home low and rush you to market, regardless of what's best for your bottom line. The faster you list, the faster they get a paycheck. Period.

Not only skimping on preparation for market, desperate agents also convince sellers to make decisions throughout the process that are against their own interests - for the purpose of selling faster so the agent can get paid, because they really need the money. Desperate agents are real, prevalent, and **toxic** to the property seller's financial interests.

If sellers screen out this type of agent early on, they'll save themselves thousands of dollars of lost profit.

There's no reason to accept representation by someone who pushes you to make decisions – about how much to list the house for, about when to list, or anything else - based on *their* need to get paid *fast*. You *deserve* to have an agent who is truly dedicated to getting you paid the *most*.

By definition, an "agent" is someone working for YOUR best interests, not theirs. Someone who represents *you* and *your* needs, not theirs. Unfortunately there are many people who call themselves "agents" but, driven by desperation, act against their clients' needs.

Don't be fooled. What's best for them is not necessarily best for you. The marketing plans they trot out are nothing more than smoke and mirrors. Their sales presentations benefit one person only – and it isn't you.

Watch out, and be aware that desperation drives a lot of what transpires in the real estate industry. Don't become the next victim! Chapter 7 will cover some specific ways that agents and companies deceive homeowners. Learning about this will help you avoid a few of the tricks of the desperate agent.

I want you to have a fantastically successful, profitable property sale. I don't want you to miss opportunities due to working with someone who isn't willing or able, or doesn't know how, to attract the highest offers to your property. This chapter has covered a few financial dangers to your transaction – and trusting in the wrong person to "help" is one of the greatest.

Make sure the agent you hire isn't driven by carelessness, ignorance, ego, or desperation, but is really working for YOU.

CHAPTER TWO

Why Shark Tank?

Studying the art of delivering the winning pitch

Watching investment-winning strategies on the show *Shark Tank* is like watching the Psychological Secrets That Sell Your Property for More acted out on TV.

Companies and real estate holdings are both tremendously valuable assets. For sellers in either asset class to reap maximum-dollar sales, they must make sure that buyers clearly understand their product's benefits and that buyers feel the investment is a good fit for them personally. The same psychology sells both companies and properties. High-value *Shark Tank* selling strategies therefore correlate directly to property selling. These strategies will elevate the everyday seller's financial status for years to come, just like they've elevated the financial status of winning *Shark Tank* entrepreneurs.

If you're not familiar with *Shark Tank*, each of the Sharks is a self-made multi-millionaire who started his or her own business and, despite odds stacked against them, reached heights of success most people never dare to dream about. Now they invest their own money in promising new businesses, products, and entrepreneurs.

The Sharks have made a lot of Regular Joes rich beyond their wildest imaginations through business partnerships secured on *Shark Tank*. Success stories are a testament to the synergy of matching a hungry everyday person with an expert investor.

Competitors who enter the Tank pitch their business to the Sharks. The presenters seek to maximize the value of their asset in the Sharks' eyes, so as to earn the best investment. The Sharks, meanwhile, want to fund competitors who operate stand-out businesses, in order to receive the greatest return on their investment. They choose to fund those presenters who offer the greatest benefits to them and who present the most overall desirable opportunities to invest.

The competitors who present on the show have poured immeasurable sweat equity, and often a lot of their own cash, into the businesses they've built. They aspire to add additional capital to their venture by garnering a Shark's investment. The goal is wild financial success for all.

How fortunate for us that in every episode, we get to study the workings of five self-made multi-millionaires in a single room! There are obvious high-value lessons right there for all to see. The lessons are free for all to watch and study - but I have yet to find anyone else applying these strategies to real estate. It's too bad, because the principles can guide anyone who watches - and pays close attention – to the secrets of reaping massive profit when selling property.

If you study the Sharks, as I have, you'll uncover their secrets. These rich, successful Sharks didn't get where they are today because they're superhuman. They, too, are regular people just like us. They just took time to investigate which elements of a business predict its success, and they've taught themselves how to identify them.

For example, they deduced that having a game plan and being well-prepared is one of the best indicators of impending success. They saw that all the best business leaders know how to value their businesses correctly and present them honestly. They determined that great entrepreneurs know how to make a great first impression, and that the safest investments are in owners who demonstrate that their product or service is already in demand.

The chapters of this book will dive deeper into the "Shark Secrets" but for starters let's focus on the top two things the Sharks demand from every competitor who pitches to them, before they'll consider investing. In my words, those demands are:

Know your product and know your value
Connect with your audience

Everyone who enters Shark Tank has decided to seek investment for something they've poured innumerable days and nights into – a product or service into which they may have invested their life savings to create. They've sacrificed countless time and money to build something they believe is very valuable. Come show time, they're ready to showcase the result of all their hard work and investment in exchange for a cash infusion from the Sharks.

The property seller is in a similar position, with the opportunity to transform all their sweat equity and property investments into real, expendable cash for themselves.

Nobody enters the Tank to take a bad deal – they've prepared long and hard for this moment - they're there to get the best Shark, the best investment, and the best terms. Likewise, a property owner shouldn't enter the selling market to settle for a raw deal – they should be purposeful, on a well-planned mission to sell their house for the greatest return on their investment.

When taking the stage, an entrepreneur will never tell the Sharks that their product is "just okay." They don't go on camera without developing a presentation worthy of investment. Same goes for home sellers. Don't go into the selling process intending to sell a property that's "just okay" – go into the market on a mission to sell a property that's great.

"But what if my house IS 'just okay'?" some may think...Or at least they fear others will think so...

The Psychological Selling Secrets propel houses of every size, every shape, and every kind to sell for maximum profit. For every property there is a buyer. When we apply our proprietary approach, we identify *in advance* what the ideal buyer for the property will be like – their pains and hopes, struggles and dreams.

We start by performing a thorough and honest assessment of both the property and the marketplace. Then we reverse-engineer the property presentation (aka listing) to speak *directly* to that buyer, in a way they can't resist. When property marketing is correctly produced, it meets the right buyers with a magnetic message crafted *specifically* for *them*, so they will recognize that *this* property is *just right* for *them*.

Let me quote something my high school choir director always told us:

Proper Preparation Prevents Poor Performance

This applies across all time and circumstance, when pitching on Shark Tank - and especially when selling real estate. By tending to the *right* details behind the scenes and leading with an incredible first impression, the presentation will succeed.

Real, human, average, everyday people compete on *Shark Tank* for the opportunity to become millionaires. Similarly, when you sell your property, you have the opportunity, should you choose to embrace it, to significantly elevate your financial status.

Winners prepare. Winners are clearly focused on the goal. Winners polish their presentations.

Losers flub up the simple things. They're unable to demonstrate why their product is worthy of investment. They put such a high price tag on their business that the Sharks will never bite.

Losers get sent packing.

Sometimes those who win a Shark's investment don't even have products that are one-of-a-kind - often they're not even the best of their kind! Rather, the winning business owners are able to secure a great investment because they know their product inside and out - how it helps people, what makes it special, and what its value is – and they convey that message impressively, in a way the Sharks respond to.

When entering the Shark Tank, the value of the business must be abundantly clear. First, in the competitor's own mind. And by the end of the presentation, the value also must be clear in the Shark's mind for the presenter to leave the Tank with a coveted Deal in hand.

Winners are those who show that their product or service fulfills a real need, and that it has already-proven demand in the market – that it has an audience, it has buyers. To get a Shark to bite, the competitor must make abundantly clear what the in-demand and investment-worthy features of the product are, so the Sharks will fall in love and, therefore, buy. Once a Shark is convinced that a business is desirable and is a good value, they jump on the deal.

Expertly leading the Sharks to see and believe in the value of the product *is* the secret of making the sale. Only well-prepared presenters communicate this For The Win. The product may not be unique or perfect, but it *must* be good and the presentation *must* be polished. The owner must communicate clearly an abundance of value. The business itself need not be perfect to win - but it's *impossible* to win without a correctly prepared presentation.

The profit is all in the planning, preparation, and presentation.

It's no different when selling property.

The advice I give to property sellers is the same as the advice I assume the Sharks would give to inventors, business owners, and presenters hoping to earn their cash:

Talk is cheap. Seeing is believing.

Know your product, know your value.

You never get a second chance to make a first impression

Everybody wants to have what everybody else wants to have.

Behind the scenes – it's where the magic happens.

Going back to true-life real estate nightmares for a moment...We regularly hear horror stories from property sellers victimized by utter recklessness at the hands of a careless agent who, for example, advertised their house at half of its actual square footage. From home owners who were horribly misrepresented and damaged by an unskilled agent's devastating mistakes drafting the counterproposal, costing *them*, the seller – not the agent who was in error - tens of thousands of dollars in lost profit. And from people who fell prey to an egotistical agent's blustery sales presentation, only to be taken advantage of in any number of ways, from underpricing the house to missing out on offers.

All these agent errors and misbehaviors completely violate the number one Shark demand: Know your product and know your value.

If there's one lesson we can all learn from *Shark Tank* – think about it as though you're about to pitch for an investment from the Sharks – it's "have a game-plan and be well-prepared". Toward that end, it's our mission to help clients Prepare Perfectly for Profitable Performance.

That doesn't mean that the property for sale has to be in perfect condition. It just means that we have a thorough and accurate understanding of both the product and the target audience, so as to generate a marketing message and property presentation that will resonate with the best buyers and get them excited about this house.

We do what's needed behind the scenes to create a presentation that makes buyers see and believe in the value of the product, starting with the very first impression, when they instinctively feel that *this* property will make their friends jealous and their family proud. By positioning and presenting the property correctly and impressively, we sell to the best buyer for maximum profit. The greatest successes aren't made by magic – it's all about proper planning, preparation, and presentation.

Just as every successful Shark Tank competitor formulates, practices, and delivers a well-crafted pitch that's unique to their product and expertly captures the Sharks' attention - in order to get the best investment, the most eager buyer, and the highest profit – so too does every property seller need The Psychological Secrets That Sell Property for More to secure the most eager, highest-paying buyer for their property.

Not unlike earning a Shark's investment, the extra profit earned by a property seller through expert application of the Psychological Selling Secrets can be life-changing indeed.

CHAPTER THREE

Psychological Selling Secret #1

Talk is Cheap. Seeing is Believing.

When an entrepreneur takes the stage telling the Sharks that his or her business is worth a million dollars, you know the Sharks will ask "So what are your sales so far?" If the entrepreneur answers "Ten thousand dollars" or some other very low or non-existent amount, he or she should prepare to be laughed off stage.

Now the business owner isn't taken seriously. They've opened their presentation by earning skepticism from the Sharks – not a good start! Instead of impressing with a fantastic product and great sales numbers, now they're a laughing stock because they've asked a ludicrous price for their company instead of a realistic value. Talk is cheap.

We'll discuss valuation in Secret #2 "Know Your Product, Know Your Value" but the point here is that you can't just *say* something without backing it up. Those who do so and expect to be hired, to be invested in, to sell a product for the highest value, will be sorely disappointed.

Just putting a million dollar price tag on a house doesn't make it *worth* a million dollars. We have to substantiate the value, first by having qualities that make it worth a million dollars, then by showcasing those qualities in a way that people can plainly see – and agree – that the house is definitively worth a million dollars, or more.

There are many important ways to incorporate this principal into effectively selling property for maximum profit. But most real estate agents don't know, much less apply, these secrets of selling. Go ahead, ask them what marketing they've studied.

I once attended a cocktail party where I was introduced to a fellow real estate agent. She shook my hand and wasted not a second before bragging that she'd been in the business for 20 years in my city and was "very successful." She worked for one of the biggest firms in the nation.

Her husband was a contractor who built homes, she said. She tried to sell his newly constructed homes to buyers. She asked me what I focus on, and I told her I specialize in marketing listings for home sellers. Her eyes crossed for a moment, as she exclaimed dramatically, "Then maybe you can help *me*! I don't know the *first* thing about marketing."

Back this up a minute, I thought. *You work for one of the largest firms in the nation. You spent the first five minutes of this conversation bragging how 'successful' you've been for 20 years. And now you tell me you don't know the first thing about marketing....*

I'm not only a direct competitor in business, mind you, but also a complete stranger. And she literally told me that she has no idea how to do her job!

I checked her sales history later and, let's just say that "highly successful" is a highly subjective descriptor. In my five years (at that time) of real estate selling experience, I had closed approximately the same number of sales as she had closed in her twenty years.

This agent is a typical specimen. There are a lot of real estate agents who, like her, have no idea how to do the job. They haven't honed a specific set of skills, highly tailored to deliver the most financially advantageous result to the home seller. They'll spend hours, if you let them, shamelessly blowing smoke about how great they are. But when you check the facts, there's *nothing* to back it up.

Maybe "their firm" does a lot of sales – but their firm may consist of hundreds of agents, the majority of whom, like the majority of real estate agents nationwide, complete fewer than five sales per year. (Yes, you read that right, the majority of licensed real estate agents complete fewer than five transactions per year.) When you add up a hundred people transacting five sales per year, it does sum up to a high total. But firm-level sales numbers say *nothing* about the experience or expertise of an individual agent. If an agent is asking to represent you by touting their *firm's* sales numbers, they may be using those figures to purposely distract you from more important information about themselves and their own experience.

If your kid told you that the class average test score was a B, would that help you in any way? Or would it only matter to you how well *your* kid specifically did on this test? It's possible your child didn't even take the test at all - maybe there were a few high-scoring students in the class, but yours didn't even turn it in. Wouldn't you want to know?

Likewise, it truly is the individual agent's quality of performance and results – not that of their firm – that affect your home sale outcome. Is the agent in front of you one who does excellent work and produces outstanding results? Or are they just another "hanger on" riding the statistical coattails of a few others at their office who do quality work?

Demand proof. Not group performance. But *individual* credentials of the specific agent who may represent you.

Applying for graduate school, I couldn't just *say* I did well in prior classwork. I had to order and have delivered to the admissions office the authentic, sealed, original transcripts directly from the source, to *prove* my credentials. The admissions office had to *see* what my work was really like. They wouldn't just take my word for it!

The Sharks simply are not going to buy in if they can't clearly see the product in action and verify that it actually works as promised. The Sharks do this to protect themselves from entering into poor, unfruitful, regrettable partnerships. If the entrepreneur isn't *already* delivering a demonstrably well-loved product or service, why should the Sharks believe that they *will*?

Talk is cheap. Seeing is believing. Property sellers will benefit from applying this principle in selecting an agent. Many agents only *tell*, often with pushy sales tactics and shameless gimmicks.

When pitching to the Sharks, you never see a contestant "guarantee" a return. If they told a Shark that they "guarantee" a certain return do you think the Shark would care? No, the Sharks aren't interested in listening to promises. They only want to see *action*. Facts. Goalposts already accomplished. Products already produced. Sales already made. If the product has been sold, ordered, and well-loved, with more orders coming in, that substantiates that this is a good investment opportunity. If the contestant proves to a Shark that their company is standing on solid ground, that their customers love them and come back for more, then the Shark will be "in".

A business owner saying "I guarantee you $XX return" would be shunned out of the room. That's just not how this works. Life isn't a guarantee. The economy differs from day to day, week to week, year to year. They simply cannot guarantee any outcome.

Similarly, if an agent tries to promise you a Guaranteed Sale Program, you too should shun them out of the room. (You do know that the guarantee sale programs are guaranteed to benefit the agent, not the seller, right? It guarantees that the agent will "get" price reductions from the seller until the price is so low the house can't possibly fail to sell. This sales strategy is *not* in the seller's favor!) Ask the agent to show you how many homes he or she has bought through the GS program. It just doesn't happen.

We believe in *showing* our sales and service credentials in the simplest and most substantiating way - with repeat and referral business. The proof is in the pudding.

Our past clients recommend and re-hire us, and it's certainly not because of some extortionary gimmick like a GSP. The experience they received through our work was superior. Attentive service. Attention to detail. Strategies for preparation, pricing, and negotiation that really work. What we offer isn't a vague promise or some gimmick developed to disadvantage homeowners. It's professional, expert service that gets superior results – in fact in many cases we get results that are better than what our clients had imagined possible.

We *want* sellers to see what our past listings and marketing look like. We *ask* sellers to review our sold listings on our website so they know what to expect. We don't hide this information. This, our portfolio – like a transcript - is proof of the quality of our work. We want people to *see* it!

Many agents purposely hide their past listings, shroud them from view like a bad dream – they're truly embarrassed by their own work.

They know that once you sign on the dotted line "you're theirs". So the fewer questions you ask and the fewer answers they have to give, the better. Once they get hired, they will slack. It's a fact - a lot of agents, once the listing contract with the seller is secure, half-ass it. I take far far too much pride in my work and my reputation to give any listing any less than the very best. But the same can't be said for many others.

When it comes to impressing home buyers, likewise we have to *show* not just *tell*, why they should buy your house. A prospective home buyer won't get excited about your property if we don't clearly *show* them specifically why this home is perfect for them. Exactly *what* about it exceeds the value of other homes they might consider? Why specifically is your property better *for them* than one down the block?

If you have beautiful hardwood floors, let's declutter so buyers can ogle them. If you've meticulously upkept the property, let's provide the maintenance records so buyers can inspect and appreciate them. If you have incredible views, let's open the curtains and trim the trees so buyers will fall in love. Whatever we're selling, let's *sell* it. Not passively make it available for sale, but actively *sell* it.

And I don't mean with gimmicks and abusive guarantee programs either. I mean with expert presentation of the listing, including top-of-the-line staging, photos, and descriptions. I mean with real, expert marketing and pricing, carefully studied, designed, and practiced over many many listings to deliver you nothing less than the very highest net profit.

We achieve exceptional client results because we obsess over the goal of *showing* buyers why they should buy your house for top dollar, exactly as the Shark Tank competitor must *show* the Sharks why they should invest in their company. Strategic implementation of a few simple property-specific enhancements amplifies the value of the product in the buyer's eyes and clearly *shows* the buyers why your home has a higher value than all the others.

Shark Tank competitors who offer nothing other than a bunch of hot air - who talk a lot but don't *show* the value of their product - get eaten alive in the Tank. They lose. Entrepreneurs who demonstrate how their product works, what's special about it, and why the Sharks should invest, get a winning deal.

Talk is cheap. Picking an agent without seeing their work is like throwing darts with your eyes closed. Make sure you know what you're really getting.

Seeing is believing. Make certain that your home's preparation, presentation, staging and marketing will effectively convey the full value of the property. This is Step One in achieving maximum profit for your property sale.

CHAPTER FOUR

Psychological Selling Secret #2

Know Your Product, Know Your Value.

"If you can't get this right, almost nothing else matters."
– Vanessa Van Edwards, The Ten Secrets to the Perfect
Shark Tank Pitch

Vanessa Van Edwards is the Lead Investigator at human behavior research lab Science of People. She's also a behavioral researcher who once watched every episode of Shark Tank, dissecting every single pitch to decipher which key elements are most important to earning an investment. While working to crack the code of how to succeed in the Tank, she discovered that, while several factors can increase the likelihood of victory, there is just one sure-fire way to *lose* - which *must* be avoided at all costs.

Van Edwards summarizes her findings in *The 10 Secrets to the Perfect Shark Tank Pitch* and elaborates in the interview "What All 495 'Shark Tank' Pitches Say About Wowing

Investors". She's owed a huge debt of gratitude for the detailed investigation she's done on this topic.

While various different advice on how to *win* can be combined for a successful pitch, Van Edwards and every other researcher on the subject are extremely emphatic that there is one absolute, clear-cut way to *lose* in the Tank. You want to get kicked out of the Shark Tank? Easy. Mess up your valuation.

Show the Sharks that you have no idea what your company is worth. Ask them to pay a completely unreasonable amount. They'll drop out like flies. They'll want nothing to do with you. Once you indicate that you don't understand your product and your value, you've lost all credibility.

To get a buyer, the owner *must* have a good sense of their company's value and be prepared to sell to the Sharks at a *reasonable* cost. When an owner lies about the business, exaggerates features, or gives a falsely inflated appearance of value, they should forget about getting a deal. In the Sharks' minds, that person can't be trusted anymore.

It's the same when selling property. Shoppers looking for a home like yours will be happy to come have a look. But once they step inside, if the asking price doesn't match the size, amenities, neighborhood, and features – they'll run away, and fast. They won't just ask for a discount. They'll save themselves the time and buy something else instead. A nonsensical list price gives the impression to home shoppers that the seller is unreasonable, possibly even untrustworthy.

In the event of a severely overpriced listing, if the seller is lucky enough to get an offer, and they accept a deal far below their asking price, then their credibility is completely shot for the rest of the negotiations. Perhaps some sellers forget or don't know, but the initial offer is not the only negotiation that transpires over the course of a property sale. There may be inspection objections, appraisal objections, and other requests from the buyer, such as extensions of time for deadlines and closing. If you have to shoot yourself in the foot to get the property under contract in the first place, plan to shoot yourself in the other foot on the way to closing.

It's critical to get the initial deal under contract without "giving away the farm" - to set the tone for ongoing interactions with the buyer.

Negotiations with the buyer begin before your property even goes to market. The conversation with the buyer starts with setting the list price. If that price is substantiated by the property's features and presentation, buyers will visit in droves and eagerly send offers. In this case, negotiations begin in the seller's favor, which is necessary to maximize profit.

When the list price doesn't match the product, credibility is lost right from the start. On a high price, the seller won't get offers. On a low price, the seller will get offers much lower than they should settle for. And either way, their negotiating power will be severely crippled. You can't negotiate effectively when the other side simply doesn't believe you.

That's why it's absolutely critical to begin the listing at an appropriate, justifiable price. By understanding the product thoroughly, as well as the market, an appropriate asking price can be set based on facts and reality, not based on puffery or falsehood. And never based on incomplete or inaccurate information, or incompetence in pricing research and analysis.

Let me give an example of how this can play out. You'll remember I mentioned in Chapter One that five agents talked to Sheila and Mike about selling their home. I visited their house and took extensive notes about its features – both good and less-than-good. It was in a very unique and desirable neighborhood, and they had remodeled much of the home. Yet, it backed to a highway, which in reality would take many buyers out of consideration. We needed to price the home correctly to maximize the value of the positives while being realistic about the negatives. After visiting their house, I returned to my desk and spent about eight hours researching various combinations of factors to determine what price I could get for them.

After the property sale was complete, I learned from Mike and Sheila that the price we sold their house for was $64,000 higher than the next highest list price that any other agent had recommended to them – and $100,000 more than the lowest.

Now's a good time to address a trick called "buying the listing" that many real estate agents play against unsuspecting – and even trusting – homeowners. This trick is explicitly forbidden by the REALTOR® Code of Ethics, but unfortunately it remains a prevalent problem nonetheless. Buying the listing is when the agent intentionally and knowingly presents to the homeowner a very high predicted sales price with the goal of being "the winning bidder" among agents interviewing to list the property. The agent has no reasonable expectation of actually selling the house for that high amount. (But of course they'll *sound* very confident at the listing presentation – they know a feigned air of certainty is necessary to gain sellers' trust.) In other words, the agent intentionally deceives the homeowner into believing that this specific agent – only - has the magic power to sell the house for a very high price, higher than anyone else can.

Once the listing agreement with the seller is signed, now this agent will get the paycheck instead of his or her competitors – because other agents presented more realistic sales prices, while this agent got the sellers to believe that he or she alone could sell the house for a lot more. Now, all he or she has to do is wait. He or she operates in expectation that eventually the home sellers will become desperate to sell and so they'll agree to reduce list price. And it will be easier to keep this listing agent, even though he or she lied to and deceived them, than to start the process over by hiring someone different. Thus by "bidding highest" on projected sales price in the beginning, this agent "won" the opportunity to list the home, while not actually being able to earn the sellers any more money than other agents.

By breaking the cardinal rule of "Know Your Product. Know Your Value," this agent makes both himself and the seller look like fools, running off potential buyers with an unreasonable list price, destroying the sellers' credibility and negotiating power in the process.

I don't "buy the listing". For Sheila and Mike – as I do for every client – I performed extensive pricing research, as much as it takes, to determine the highest sales price that I can justify based on the product's real features and benefits, and limited by its weaknesses. I know that our expert marketing will make the property look its best, and our negotiating strategies will ensure a great contract for the seller. I just have to invest the time and analytical skill into thorough pricing research, and we'll achieve a maximum-profit sale.

In Sheila and Mike's case, my research bore out the fact that due to all its hard-to-find positive attributes, we could still sell this house for top dollar, despite the highway behind it. Other agents either didn't invest enough time to do sufficient research, didn't know how to correctly analyze such a unique property, or decided to intentionally recommend underpricing the home because they were afraid they couldn't sell it any other way.

On the opposite end of the spectrum from "buying the listing" is the other trick that real estate agents commonly use, which is to "beat up the property" and intentionally lowball the value. If you imagine going to sell your vehicle to a used car lot, it's much like that. In the first meeting with a seller, the agent will view the home in detail, with one goal in mind - to "beat up", or disparage, many facets of the property as they tour through. They aren't just being objective, they're purposely exaggerating and inventing negative features to put you in a low-price state of mind and lead you to believe that your property's value is lower than others.

Agents who engage in this practice of beating up the property intentionally set the seller's expectations very low and then assign the house a lower list price than it deserves. They do this for three main reasons: 1) So they can sell the property very fast, thus having to do less work. 2) So they don't have to invest any time or money into real marketing that attracts top-dollar buyers. 3) And so they don't have to put in any effort or skill into negotiating for their client at contract time. In other words, pricing their listings very low saves them tons of time and work.

These agents do minimal market research, put little or no effort into property marketing - they even fail their client in negotiations - and in the end, they get a bare minimum price contract for their sellers.

Well-known and "very successful" agents can be especially guilty of this. Because their name is very recognizable, people assume them to be very knowledgeable. So sellers are *more likely* to accept a low valuation from a well-known agent, due to the perception of the agent's authority. Such agents routinely exploit this perception and price their listing low, taking advantage of the seller's trust in their price opinion.

Once the property is listed at a low price, the agent doesn't have to think, and they don't have to try. They "just throw it on the market" as they say, and it will automatically sell because it's priced so low. This is a great deal for the agent, who still gets paid for transacting the sale with minimal effort, and it's a horrible deal for sellers who lose many thousands of dollars in profit - oftentimes without ever knowing it.

I presented my recommended price to Sheila and Mike, and other agents presented theirs. I presented my evidence for my valuation. I don't know what evidence others may have presented. But because Sheila and Mike could see that I knew the product and I knew the value, they hired me, and then I sold their house for $64,000-$1000,000 more than any other agent said they could. THIS is the value of knowing your product and knowing your value.

When your agent takes time to get to know your property very well – both the pros and cons of it – *and* they take their time to evaluate its value correctly, your list price will make serious buyers come running to see the house and rush to submit good offers. When we work these offers with skilled negotiation, backed up by credibility that comes from accurately representing the property and its value, it's the recipe for maximum profit.

If an agent arrives at your house with a list price already picked out for you before they've even been inside the home, shoo them away.

The only way to do proper research and deliver the most profitable result is to perform the pricing research *after* we've been able to see inside the house, and after we consider any upcoming changes. Not every home needs improvements, and not every seller is able to do improvements. That's perfectly ok. We just need to assign the list price based on the actual facts of the property, not guesses made before touring the house.

Entrepreneurs who ask an unsupported value for their products on Shark Tank get laughed off stage, humiliated. They leave empty-handed. Same happens to sellers who pitch an incorrectly priced listing to the market. Both over- and under-pricing a property can cost the seller tens of thousands of dollars.

"If you can't get this right, almost nothing else matters."

Don't let somebody buy your listing with false promises. Don't let them beat up the property and scare you into underpricing. Make sure you and your agent both thoroughly know the product and the value. When you go to market with an asking price that's attractive to serious buyers, you'll walk away with a winning deal and a *big* smile on your face.

CHAPTER FIVE

Psychological Selling Secret #3

You Never Get a Second Chance to Make a First Impression.

"People won't remember what you said or what you did. They'll remember how you made them feel."
- attributed to Carl W. Buehner, Frank A. Patterson, Maya Angelou, and others - original author undetermined

Making that emotional connection with the audience proves over and over again its effectiveness – yes, necessity – in sales of all kinds. We must make them *feel* something!

"The entrepreneurs who smiled broadly and then nodded at the sharks before starting their pitch were much more likely to have a successful interaction. In fact, the smile and nod almost doubled the chances of getting a 'yes'..." – *The Ten Secrets to the Perfect Shark Tank Pitch*

This works too in home selling!

When entering the Tank, a business owner must come through the doors with a *bang*. He or she must Wow the investors. A shocking demo, a tragic problem, a never-before-seen performance - something special *must* happen in those first crucial moments to forge a meaningful, unshakeable connection with the Sharks. *The Ten Secrets to the Perfect Shark Tank Pitch* reports that Emotional Buy-In from a Shark correlates highly to earning their investment. The Sharks who give a deal are usually "hooked", meaning emotionally involved in the entrepreneur's story. The First Impression is the ideal time to make that emotional connection.

You too, as a property seller, get only one chance to make a first impression – so make it a good one!

Psychology says the first impression occurs in the first 1-3 seconds. And you can't take it back. Neurological hard-wiring in the limbic system of the brain makes people completely unable to ignore their initial gut instinct – whatever that may be – much as their logical mind might wish them to feel otherwise. So let's capitalize on this!

Even if a couple of Shark Tank business opportunities are similar or equally good, not every business owner presents their product in a way that's equally compelling – and this matters a great deal in who wins a Shark's investment. Not all *presentations* are created equal.

A dull presentation of even a decent product doesn't get buyers excited – it doesn't make them open their wallets. It doesn't entice them to throw their cash on the table. But an excellent presentation does.

What do the best entrepreneurs do in the opening moments of their presentation? They tell a captivating story. The specific product matters *only* after people care about your story.

Two different entrepreneurs may pitch two great new lines of sportswear to the Sharks, but the Sharks pay top-dollar for one and send the other packing, with no deal at all! What's the difference? Oftentimes, it's the quality of the presentation. To be successful, one must not underestimate the power of the First Impression.

Think about selling your home as an investment pitch. If you want people to buy your house - your product - at premium pricing...if you want them to invest their money in what you're selling, on the best terms for you, then it's simple: We already know from Psychological Selling Secret #1 that we must *show* the potential investor *why* they should want what we're selling, and from Psychological Selling Secret #2 that we must substantiate the value we assign to it...

Psychological Selling Secret #3 is that we must connect strongly with the potential buyer by making an excellent first impression – communicate to them how they'll *feel* living in this home. Remove all barriers that could impede them from appreciating the positives. Flaunt the best features in a way that will resonate with them and connect with them on a personal level. Make them *feel* how *this* house will make their lives better.

The Grand Entrance

To win on Shark Tank, the most important thing an entrepreneur can do is to smile and nod, and acknowledge the audience - the Sharks.

Likewise, acknowledge the people who are coming to see your house. Show that you respect them and you appreciate them coming to see your property. Conveying this message requires attention to detail in the first impression.

For an entrepreneur to walk into the Shark Tank and give a basic product demo, outline product features, show a few charts, and share sales data...and expect to secure a good investment from the Sharks...is just not realistic. It's incumbent upon the party with something to sell to *impress* the people who may consider buying it, to demonstrate how the product will solve their problems and make their lives better.

People are shopping for so much more than just a roof and four walls. They're searching for a dream – a place that brings the home they've imagined in their minds to life. A place that solves their problems and offers them that "special something" that other homes lack. Giving that to them will maximize your property's sale price.

Solving Pain Points

People who are moving are characterized by having at least one of a common set of problems that they need to move *away* from – in other words, their pain points. Just as every successful Shark Tank pitch has focused on solving a specific problem – a specific pain point - we position each seller's property to solve certain pain points that are characteristic of their potential buyer's lives. (In Psychological Selling Secret #5 we'll dive into more detail about how to identify and sell to the specific property's target audience.)

When the seller prepares and positions the product according to the principles of Psychological Selling Secret #3, the target buyer will immediately feel, perhaps even against the hesitations of their logical mind, that here – in this specific property – they'll escape their pains and their problems. And that *feeling* portends financial success for the property owner in the sale.

Toward this goal, little things mean a lot. We have methods for manipulating value. We need to position *your* property as the solution to the buyer's problems. As any entrepreneur knows, before entering the Tank, strategic steps should be taken to manipulate and improve product value before pitching the investment opportunity. Attention to detail pays off.

Manipulating Value

When preparing to take a seller's listing to market, most agents, unfortunately, rush the process (as discussed back in Chapter Three) - they pay no mind to the Psychological Selling Secrets, much less take time to help sellers implement them. So their seller clients fail to capitalize fully on their home sale. By applying Psychological Selling Secret #3, everything changes.

Just as various similar products have been presented on Shark Tank over time, yet only the ones that resonate with the Sharks win, so too can we gain massive improvements in your net profit by tweaking that first impression – by making small, critical changes to wow visitors and produce an unshakeable emotional connection with them immediately.

Don't make pricing decisions based solely on "comps." You don't have to believe that just because the house down the block sold for a certain price that yours will too. Many agents oversimplify this aspect of pricing a house. Making a few seemingly minor but psychologically impactful improvements in your home's presentation will forge a stronger connection with your audience – the home shoppers, your prospective buyers - so the value of your property increases in their eyes. You'll walk away with a great deal, while your neighbor won't.

Pricing should be calculated based on market conditions, the home's unique features, *and* the property's presentation. There's tremendous value in presentation. Value that many agents and their sellers fail to tap. For the highest return on investment, make sure to tap into this wellspring.

Let me give an example. A brown lawn can be professionally revived for a few thousand dollars or less. Yet, that brown lawn can drag down the home's sale price by as much as 14%. That means for a $300,000 home, the investment of a few thousand dollars to bring the lawn back to a healthy green can potentially earn you a profit return of over $30,000. This is far from the only example. It's just one way to put this method into practice.

When you're about to sell your car, you'd clean it and spruce it up before driving over to the dealer's lot, so that you can get the best offer. Similarly, to capitalize on the power of the First Impression, if there are things about the property you want to sell that are broken which you can fix, fix them! The key to achieving maximum profit is to increase both actual and perceived value.

Think about a home's front stoop. When concrete's crumbling underfoot, front door covered in dust, screen ripped, and cobwebs growing around the light fixture, no one will imagine inviting friends here for a housewarming! But after the seller invests a couple of hours spit-shining the entry, washing the door, replacing the screen, cleaning the light, suddenly aspiring new homeowners feel happy when they approach – they're eager to see inside – they'd be proud to bring guests to *this* house. This house makes them feel *welcome* and *at home*.

What's the value of that *feeling*? The feeling of *home*? Where they can picture themselves throwing a jubilant housewarming party next month. They can imagine family members arriving one-by-one for Thanksgiving dinner, holding their dishes, standing in this same spot, also feeling welcome and at home, and proud to be here.

No one wants to think about Thanksgiving Day with family greeted by a crumbling porch, dirty door, ripped screen, and cobwebs. They, the buyers - all of them, every single one - want a peaceful, clean, welcoming entry that makes them feel at home. And they *will* pay more for it (even if they think they don't want to).

So preparing a home for listing is about generating a feeling of pride in potential buyers, but it's also about how it will make the buyer's friends and family feel. If buyers feel it will make their friends jealous and their family proud, *that's* the feeling they will clamor for, and fight for, and pay top-dollar for. Not only to feel proud for themselves but also to show off to others.

People love to be admired, and if they get the chance to purchase a property that will make others admire them, indeed even jealous of them, they will pay more for that.

Applying this concept in just one location on the property can add thousands of dollars to your sale price. Applying it all around the property can add tens of thousands of dollars.

This is how rich, successful investors like the Sharks think.

The Sharks decide on their investments based upon potential return as well as the business leader's skill at communicating a product's value. Similarly, our goal is to impress the audience of home shoppers and expertly communicate the home's value. As you'll read more in Psychological Selling Secret #4, everybody wants to have what everybody else wants to have, which is to say that when a potential buyer's first impression is "My friends will wish they had a house like this!" then your sale is imminent.

Impressive things are valuable both because the buyer is personally impressed by them, and also because they know it will impress others – and the desire to impress others is one of the strongest psychological motives in purchase decisions.

How to Design a Winning First Impression

Through presentation, you get the chance to elevate your property's sale price in a positive way to yield greater profit. You'll want to make sure that the agent you work with evaluates your property according to the Psychological Selling Secrets and provides you with expert guidance to maximize both the property's appeal and the price that buyers will pay.

I advise sellers on how to prepare and position their home as the solution to their target audience's pain points. This preparation begins with eliminating specific property flaws where possible and strategically enhancing key profit-elevating features. Then we build marketing for the house that psychologically primes the audience to want to bite on this opportunity. Finally, we ensure that upon arrival - before logical thought has time to kick in - when the buyer has consciously noticed nothing more than the fact that they've arrived - they will *feel* something. If they feel *at home*, we're on our way to a high-dollar deal!

When touring our clients' homes, we evaluate many seemingly minor details about each house to identify places where making a minor change - often costing only $50 or nothing at all – can return the seller thousands in profit on the sale price. Certain ostensibly minor changes will markedly improve the property's perceived value. Our proprietary method in part involves advising sellers on such seemingly small, but actually very powerful, opportunities to add real value to their properties at little or no cost to themselves.

Home shoppers may not have *wanted* to pay top dollar for a home. But once they see your house, which *impressed* them so much, now they want your house more than they want the money they would have saved by buying something less impressive.

Make sense?

Our proprietary psychological strategy evaluates each home's presentation on fourteen psychological selling parameters.

By implementing a value-add strategy like the Sharks - highly successful and well-compensated investors - and understanding how to impress people in the first moments, the value of your property will be maximized, as will your return on investment.

People are driven by unseen, hard-wired psychological forces in their purchase decisions. We take advantage of this knowledge and manipulate these psychological forces through our Selling Secrets to increase the price people will pay for your property.

By analyzing fourteen different factors, we capitalize on the uptapped potential in any property to maximize profit. When we Wow the buyers right out of the gate, they have no power to say "no" to your property, even if they wanted to.

This is why you never want to skip on preparation. *This* is a great place to make money! With that very first step – that *best foot forward*.

When the buyer sees – no, not just sees – but when they can *feel* that you're excited to present this house to them and you're making an effort to impress them, they become so much more inclined to willingly, happily, emphatically buy. At this point, the price it costs them to get this home is a *secondary* concern to how you've made them *feel*.

Now they *need* to have what you're selling. They *need* to live here. Because you have wowed them.

It's a feeling they cannot shake.

CHAPTER SIX

Psychological Selling Secret #4

Everybody Wants to Have What Everybody Else Wants to Have.

Why was an eight-inch plush toy selling for thousands of dollars in the late 1990's?

Why did 300 people stampede a Wal-Mart, trampling an employee, to buy a giggling red doll in 1996?

It's the same reason fashion trends come and go. The same reason diet and exercise trends come and go.

It's the basic psychological principle that humans want to have what everyone else wants to have.

Most people don't even need a personal reason for wanting to purchase something – "Everybody else is into it!" is good enough.

Beanie Babies. Tickle Me Elmo. They're a drop in the bucket.

Do you remember the year that Billy Blank's Tae Bo videos were all the rage? How many copycat kickboxing-fitness videotapes came out that year? A lot. Why?

Because suddenly kickboxing fitness videos became the *in* thing. Everybody wanted to have one because everybody else wanted to have one. So it suddenly became *the* easiest product in the world to sell. And for the product sellers, it was the *easiest* way to make money.

There was *demand* for kickboxing fitness videos – heavy demand. Not because scientific studies had recently proved it superior for weight loss. Not because it's the world's greatest form of self-defense. Not for any reason other than it "caught on." People wanted it because everybody else they knew wanted it. Simple as that.

In the supply-and-demand equation, it's demand that tells us *what* to deliver to the market, in order to sell for maximum profit.

Essentially demand is everyone wanting the same thing at the same time.

The human psyche is such that people look around and see what everybody else wants, has, or is trying to get. When they perceive that all their peers are wanting the same thing, they assume that thing to be valuable. It suddenly feels like something that they, too, need and ought to have - therefore they decide that they want to buy it too.

To maximize profit, then, we simply make the connection between what you're selling and what everybody else wants right now. As the Sharks always ask, "Do you have sales?"

To the Sharks, ideally the entrepreneur has already *proved* demand for their product through a healthy sales record. On Shark Tank, inventing something that people find interesting isn't enough – the entrepreneur needs to invent something that consumers actually purchase. Once a business owner proves that many people have already bought their product, then logically, many more people are expected to desire and pay for the item too. Basic human psychology.

That's where we tap into maximum profits.

How do we do this for the property seller? The property seller, it would seem, is in a different circumstance altogether, having a supply of only one to sell, after all.

In this special case of selling a property, supply of one, we need to make the correlation between what property *features* are currently most in-demand (and therefore profitable) in the local market, and what features you have in your house. We position your property into this profitable stream of demand by playing up the popular features you already have. We make certain that what people crave most will stand out during showings at your house, and we prominently showcase the coveted elements in our marketing. Because certain features have current, provable demand in the local market – we can see that they've been selling faster and for more money – then we know that more home shoppers will covet these features in your home too and will be eager to pay for them.

If the property's current qualities aren't already popular, we can still generate demand by adding a few strategically selected features. Adding to your property a few additional aspects in common with the most highly sought-after homes in your marketplace is great way to attract demand and the extra profit that comes with it.

Some in-demand features can be added quickly, easily, and affordably to most properties. It can be as simple as adding expert home staging to start increasing net profit. Changing light fixtures and cabinet pulls can quickly modernize the look on just a minor budget. Some folks are lucky enough to be able to simply remove the old carpet and reveal original wood floors, increasing value by $10,000 in the blink of an eye.

Whether it's strategically removing a certain wall, or selectively repainting a couple of rooms, we can evaluate any home to recommend the best small projects for tapping into the "Everybody wants to have what everybody else wants to have" Psychological Selling Secret.

We may see, for example, that homes of the same size as yours with new carpet sold for an average of $10,000 more than similar homes with old carpet, and the updated ones sold five times faster too. So if new carpet for your house costs $4,000 to install, then this will be a profitable improvement. If you're able to make the up-front investment, it will be worth doing. Knowing the facts, you can then confidently take advantage of this opportunity for a faster, higher-dollar sale.

The key is to accurately identify the most highly-craved property characteristics that both offer you a great return on your investment and that are within your means to incorporate or highlight in your property. This often involves making important financial decisions about where to strategically invest, while identifying and avoiding potential changes that wouldn't produce a justifiable return.

With your specific in-demand features spruced up, added, and highlighted, we attract competition for your product, a supply of just one, among a demand of many, so you'll sell for maximum profit.

Have you ever seen the Sharks argue and compete with one another to buy into a business? This is where life-changing success can happen for the business owner. This seller gets to *choose* which Shark they prefer to work with – their favorite, the greatest expert in their particular field, the one who offers the most benefits and the most favorable terms to them. No longer are they at the whim of whichever one Shark might like them – now they get their pick of the Sharks, and they can leverage the competition among buyers to secure the best possible investment.

We use this strategy in home-selling too.

When we tap into the psyche of the public, extrapolating what they most demand and applying it to your property, we sell very profitably by attracting competition among buyers.

Now *you* get to pick the buyer who offers you the most benefits and the most favorable terms.

Like being the only seller of a coveted Beanie Baby or Tickle Me Elmo in the mid-'90s, when we activate Psychological Selling Secret #4 to demonstrate that what you're selling is what everyone wants, then we can pit the buyers against one another for your attention, extracting maximum value from your property.

CHAPTER SEVEN

Psychological Selling Secret #5

Behind the Scenes – It's Where the Magic Happens.

Every Shark Tank pitch, as shown on TV, is cut and trimmed to feature each presentation for about six minutes apiece.

The real-life pitch and ensuing conversation with the Sharks actually run much longer, sometimes over an hour. Before making a financial investment, the Sharks have to get familiar with the product, business, sale volume, and leadership of the company. They ask question after question, grilling the business owner for all the details. The real-life investment process is very in-depth and takes quite a bit of time, even though post-production editing makes it appear simple and straightforward to the TV-watching audience.

Once a Shark agrees to buy into a company on the show, the deal isn't finalized yet. After the show wraps, the Shark enters into a thorough due diligence process, digging deeper to uncover every fact and facet of the company and its finances, good and bad, before the deal is truly finalized.

The Shark is a business expert. And experts do their research. They investigate, ask good questions, and make sure they fully understand the investment before getting financially involved.

Similarly, a serious listing agent needs to get a firm and complete understanding of a property – both the good and bad - the unique features and benefits, and any repair items, before putting it on market. They need to understand the personal needs of the seller and occupants of the home, including communication preferences, showing restrictions, and other situation specifics that will affect the transaction.

Meanwhile, the seller needs to get a complete and thorough understanding of the agent. Plenty of shady salesmen have taken the Shark Tank stage to pitch sub-par products and mediocre services. What do they do? Many of the same things that pushy, unsophisticated real estate agents will do.

They heap on extra hype to *try* and skirt any discussion of the very real deficiencies in what they're selling.

They hate questions and love to respond with vague but upbeat responses like "Just wait and see – you're gonna love it, I promise." ...without telling *how* they'll achieve their "amazing" results.

Another trick that slick salespeople use is to proceed very fast, skipping the details to move as quickly as possible to the moment when you agree to buy what they're selling. Preferring to perform their whole song-and-dance question-free, they mix a few actual facts with utter hype and deception to make the service sound great. But once actually you place your order for what they're selling, watch out...my how things will change.

This type of salesperson is a trickster – so long as only their hands are turning the slides, so long as they control the conversation and no one else, they can make themselves and their product appear flawless.

But as soon as you sign on the dotted line, the show falls apart, the service fails to deliver as promised – in short, it's a total letdown, or worse.

Don't let this happen to you. Get behind the scenes.

Insider Secrets

I'm about to let the cat out of the bag here that many agents – and large well-known firms - will be livid about...Like they got caught with their pants down...trying to tug them up as fast as they can, telling you "You didn't see that."

We're pulling back the curtain on the Wizard of Oz.

A favorite strategy the bad apples use to deceive is "their numbers."

"But wait!" I can hear in many minds right now. "The numbers don't lie!"

Unfortunately, in certain hands, they do. Pushy salespeople use "their numbers" to exaggerate their services and their effectiveness. Statistics, "properly misused," provide a great tool for their sleight-of-hand.

Perhaps you've heard of, or read, the book *How to Lie with Statistics* by Darrell Huff. Written in 1954, it's more relevant today than ever. It explains exactly how statistics can be manipulated, distorting conclusions and exaggerating comparisons. The misuses of data, as detailed in that book, have been the bread and butter of a certain type of salesperson since time immemorial.

One of the book's themes, discarded data, is widely prevalent among real estate agents' self-presented statistics. Behind the scenes, they can select only their most successful sales to put in their charts and graphs, rather than *all* their sales, and no one would ever know. It's all in *which* numbers they choose to use, and how it's organized.

It's extraordinarily simple to discard data. A few second's click of a mouse unchecks less-than stellar listing attempts, excluding poor sales figures from the data set. With that single sleight-of-hand, voilá, a near-perfect sales chart! It's now missing a few imperfect listing records – and no one will ever know. Discarded data. Easy.

Suffice it to say, statistics can be, and frequently are, manipulated. Made to say almost anything someone wants them to say. I'll give a few examples in just a moment. But first let me mention, the one thing that sales numbers will never reveal is whether an agent's past clients were happy with the sales process, the service, and the outcome of their sale. And this information is a much better predictor of what your sale process will be like than are numbers like the agent's volume of properties sold or average property sale price.

Another tactic unveiled in *How to Lie* is that "If you can't prove what you want to prove, demonstrate something else and pretend they are the same thing." Agents *love* to brag about their "best-in-office" sales, or high percentage of this or that they've accumulated – but the agent's obsession with these numbers actually can have unanticipated *negative* implications on you and your profit. As you'll see in the examples that follow, success for the agent *isn't* the same thing as success for the seller.

One popular statistic (and if you've never heard of this, you're probably better for it...) is the "Sale Price to List Price Ratio". It's a number showing whether or not the agent generally sells their listings for full asking price. Sounds good, right? That's why it's a really popular statistic for agents to tout.

But let me tell you how this statistic works behind the scenes and how it can affect you, the individual seller. Many an agent, to keep this number nice and high for their sales charts, simply tells you that you must list your property at a lower price! "With low expectations, you'll never be disappointed," as the theory goes.

By setting the bar (aka asking price) low, the property is guaranteed to sell for *full* list price...because the recommended list price is *less than the full value of what the home is worth*! How does that sound to you, for the sale of your home? Do you want the most available profit, or just enough for the agent to hit their sales numbers?

And they're very convincing too – like used car salesmen, beating up the car you're trading in – suddenly every little thing is wrong with it, and instead of giving you an honest value, they lowball you on price and then throw the vehicle back out on the floor for a quick sale. Easy in, easy out, and they look great.

Real estate agents do this *all* the time – they convince sellers to list at what they know to be a low price in order to preserve the agent's precious "numbers", all to accompany their next listing presentation.

Here's another statistic that *sounds* great...until you think about how it can affect you. (You know the best lie is mostly truth, right?...) "Days on Market." Less is better, right? We can all agree that generally a fast, easy sale is nice.

But often behind the curtain of the "perfect sales numbers" is the reality – to keep their Days on Market track record looking good, the agent is pressuring homeowners to reduce price and accept low offers. That's an awfully steep penalty for innocent home sellers to pay so that these agents can keep their numbers looking "just so" on the sales charts, don't you agree?

I always present clients with a minimum price figure, a number that I'm certain in the current conditions will sell the property quickly. If the sellers must be out of the property immediately, that's the price we should go with...*but*...not every scenario is best addressed with minimum pricing. If a property has some special features, and we know who our target audience is and what premium that target audience will pay for the luxury of those features – then we price the property accordingly. (We'll cover this in more depth at the end of this chapter.) Sometimes, it takes a little more time to get the perfect buyer for a specific set of features. But if the right buyer is willing to pay $10,000 to $50,000 above minimum pricing, for many sellers that's worth a little wait.

I don't lowball sellers' list price or force price reductions to keep my "numbers" looking perfect. I work for each individual as an individual, and the selling strategy we use for each client is uniquely tailored to them and their needs.

Providing individualized, tailored service to each seller is far more important to me than "the numbers".

If you want to feel like a number, a faceless cog in a wheel, then work with an agent who's obsessed with "their numbers" – because that's exactly what will happen.

One final number that sounds good, but can actually be a detriment to the individual seller, is the agent's total number of deals closed. Sure, you want someone with experience – usually the more the better. And you want someone who's actively selling - someone who's in touch with the pulse of the market because they work in it every day. But there can be too much of a good thing.

The agent with the "highest sales volume" won't be too busy to pitch you their sales presentation. But as soon as you sign up, what happens? You almost never speak with the agent who's "representing" you again. They're off doing more sales presentations to other sellers around town while assistants field your phone calls. That agent certainly won't have time to tailor your listing strategy to *your* needs, because they're out working on *their* need to list the most houses in the city. When it's time to negotiate an offer, will they sit with you, take the time necessary, and really negotiate the *best* deal for you?

Paying attention to not just numbers, but also agent reviews can help separate fact from fiction. How was the *experience* for people who worked with the agent? How many of their clients would recommend the agent? One or two reviews just means they have a few friends. Really digging to find out what *most* clients thought of the service can save a lot of pain later.

Did the seller get the information they needed? Did they feel like they mattered? Were they able to reach the agent when they had questions? Before marketing the home, did the agent advise the seller on the psychological factors that will sell their home for the highest profit?

Every one of the fourteen psychological secrets is an opportunity to capitalize on untapped earning potential of your house. These principles operate behind the scenes. So buyers don't even know what's happened, they just know they *love* the house. Most agents never realize how much money their clients are missing out on. Although they see certain listings selling for higher prices "for no apparent reason", they never bother to learn how to do this for their own clients!

And here's just one more secret...You don't even need to utilize all fourteen psychological selling secrets to tap into extra profits. Tactfully and correctly bringing just a few of them into play behind the scenes can earn sellers an extra $40,000 or more.

Speak to the Right Audience

With an eye on Shark Tank investment trends, we can apply the pitch strategies that *really* work to sell your house for the greatest profit. Borrowing from studies of the most successful marketers to pitch on Shark Tank, to sell a house for top dollar, we too *must* know the audience.

Let's look at Psychological Selling Secret #5 at work behind the scenes...

The Sharks invest based on what fits their needs, wants, abilities, and lifestyle. Damon John is interested in clothing-related brands, and Robert Herjavec is great with tech stuff. Barbara Corcoran buys up the real estate deals. Kevin O'Leary likes products related to wine. While Mark Cuban never invests in pet products, Lori Greiner loves to invest in gadgets that will sell on QVC and in Bed Bath and Beyond, especially ones for women. You have to know your audience.

A business owner selling an apparel line would want to study Damon, wouldn't they? Walk in and smile at him. Make sure to give him a gift that he'll love. Make eye contact especially with him during the presentation.

If they want to sell their product on QVC, they'd study past episodes and see what endears Lori to an entrepreneur. What does she want to see and hear? Then they'd do that when they take the stage. And if they've designed a pet product, they shouldn't waste their time pitching to Mark – it won't go anywhere – so they should focus their efforts on the Sharks who *do* comprise their audience of potential buyers.

To effectively sell anything, then, we must begin by identifying *who* we will sell it to. One can't make a sale without connecting with an interested buyer, so determining in advance *who* the likely buyer will be – and building marketing designed to attract them - is critical.

Who will have the greatest need, desire, and appreciation for the product? What's that person like? When they come to view the property, *what* will they most appreciate? What will they demand? What will they want to see? What will excite them? What will WOW them?

After identifying what the highest-paying buyer will be like, *then* preparation of the property will be tailored to that buyer's tastes. Pricing and marketing are designed for *that* buyer's eye, customized to make sure they will clearly see the unique benefits that this home offers to their life.

Know who you're pitching to – know what they need to see and what they demand. When you deliver that, they'll quickly and eagerly pay the highest price. Just like the Sharks do for an exceptional product pitch, the buyers will jump up out of their seats, argue, fight and overbid to get the thing that appeals to them and their tastes. This is a very real phenomenon, and it's the gold standard we strive for!

Once we identify your ideal investor, we can tailor your property and its marketing to that target audience and show them the value that they've been searching for. They'll be excited to jump on it.

That's what expert marketing is all about.

Not smoke and mirrors.

Not sleight of hand.

Rather, it's the system of appearing to get inside the head of your target audience (buyer) and thus "miraculously" delivering exactly what they want to see.

It's actually not magic at all – it's science. The science of psychological selling. And it works.

It works what "appear" to the untrained eye to be miracles (which is cool!). Really it's all in what happens Behind the Scenes – and much of this is well within the seller's and agent's control to manipulate, change, and improve, to achieve the greatest profit upon sale.

Make sure *you're* working with someone who's not fixated on their superficial, manipulated, or misleading sales "numbers", unless you prefer to be – and are ready to become – Just Another Number on his or her next sales chart.

Work with someone who knows the science of real, effective preparation and of calculated, professional marketing – someone who will apply the Psychological Selling Secrets for you.

CHAPTER EIGHT

Winners vs Losers

I wrote this book for *you* and for *your* success.

I want you - like my best friend pitching on Shark Tank - to secure the highest possible investment when selling your property. There are a few things in this book you've probably heard before and a few you haven't. I've curated them all together because together in concert they produce wild success.

Some statements I've made in this book address specific underhanded tactics employed by some agents, and you may not have heard such direct comments before. There's a reason that these truths, which present a real and present danger to you as a home seller, stay hidden and hushed. I must warn you though, it's not a good reason...

Virtually never will one Realtor publicly print disparaging information about other Realtors. You'll especially not see them reveal the Insider Tricks. Every agent knows these tricks, and I believe that if they're not working to stop them, then they're complicit in making sure that innocent home sellers who rely on us remain in the dark, in danger, never knowing what to look out for or how to protect themselves.

Why would a good Realtor, who knows that agents often employ certain underhanded practices to shortchange property sellers, never disseminate this information to protect the public???

Call it a gag order, or a threat, or whatever you like, but here's what's happening...

New Realtors receive instruction on the National Association of Realtors Code of Ethics. Generally speaking, that's a very good thing. In this training, new agents get a primer on many important ethical standards. But the teaching of one specific line in the code of ethics leads to the shrouding of devious and destructive practices by real estate agents. The teaching of this rule forces a complicit silence among Realtors who know better - enabling the bad apples to continue their damaging misbehavior.

Many firms and trainings teach their brokers "Don't speak negatively about other agents – that's an Article 15 violation," referring to Article 15 of the NAR Code of Ethics. The teaching of the "Article 15 rule" hushes the truth-tellers and prevents information about some of the unseemly agent tricks I've shared in this book from being brought out into the light of day.

What I've written, when negative about other agents and firms, is not untrue. It's factual. And these are facts that you deserve to know about. Malpractice. Deceit. Ignorance. Apathy. Things that affect you, that can deeply affect your financial future – they need to be called out and stopped.

In all fairness, here's what Article 15 *actually* says: "Realtors shall not knowingly or recklessly make false or misleading statements about other real estate professionals, their businesses, or their business practices." That imperative, like all ethics rules, makes intuitive sense. Don't lie about others.

But, right or wrong, Article 15 is widely taught, construed, and interpreted throughout the industry as "Don't say *anything* negative about other agents." The result: a perceived and practiced gag order against truth-telling - such as some of what you've read in this book - against other agents' unsavory practices. When a well-meaning agent is told they'll get in trouble if they say something negative about other real estate agents, what do you think they'll do? Talk about the issues and fight them publicly? Or keep quiet so they don't risk getting in trouble?

Some of what you've just read in this book is therefore a bit more shocking than you might be used to. It's also more true, more accurate. If those who wish to do harm continue doing harm, and those who wish to do good are afraid to say anything about the others for risk of losing their own livelihoods, what prevails – truth or lies? We need voices "from the inside" to speak out about the dangers to home sellers, as one understands them best when seeing them played out on a daily basis.

Article 15 also includes the obligation "to not knowingly or recklessly publish, repeat, retransmit, or republish false or misleading statements made by others." Fair enough – don't repeat lies. But do repeat truths!

Certain parties repeat mistruths emphatically, knowing that the more frequently something is heard the more real it sounds. Don't believe it.

Mark Twain wrote, "It's easier to fool someone than to convince them that they have been fooled."

Try thinking of Mark Twain's quote if you're experiencing an agent trying to rush you to sign and "list now!" before you're ready.

If an agent's "numbers" become the main focus of your conversation, instead of *your* house and *your* specific needs. If someone's telling you that your property is bound to sell at just one fixed price no matter what you do. And if low-service agents and agencies have got you thinking that a one-size fits all approach will be equally profitable for you as a psychological marketing plan customized to your house. Remember what Mark Twain said.

There's a range of values for every property. You can sell on the high side or on the low side of the range, and that difference can easily be in excess of $40,000. The decisions you make between now and then make all the difference. Getting experienced, competent guidance about the best preparations for your specific property is a great place to start.

Home sellers deserve access to this information, without which they stand to lose a small fortune. You have the right to know what problems can affect you if you're not careful. You have the right to understand *all* the factors that keep some properties selling on the low end of the range, and what will help *your* property sell on the highest side of the range.

Use your own instinct when you decide what to believe. Protect yourself, and know that there are ways to get the profit you deserve out of your property sale – without involving braggart, pushy, or low-service agents.

In 2014 the National Association of Realtors commissioned an in-depth study. According to the project website, the goal of the report was to provide "a comprehensive and objective analysis of the most significant dangers and risks that could possibly impact the industry." They created a national Strategic Thinking Advisory Committee and hired a leading management-consulting firm. They culled 7,899 survey responses and conducted interviews with 70 industry thought leaders. The result was a 164-page report.

After all that work, NAR released the report so quietly in 2015. Did they not want anyone to read it? Very few even know it exists. The report is grandiosely titled the "definitive analysis of negative game changers emerging in real estate", or *D.A.N.G.E.R. REPORT*, and I'll be shocked if you or anyone you know has ever heard of it. After all that time – and certainly money – invested to commission a comprehensive, professionally researched report, why oh why has it been hush-hushed? Kept in the dark? Swept under the rug?

Let me venture a hypothesis.

The Report features five sections A through E, each having ten subheadings, each of which outlines one danger. Out of 50 identified industry dangers, section A item #1 is titled in bold, all-capital font:

"MASSES OF MARGINAL AGENTS DESTROY REPUTATION"

That is Danger A1 of the NAR commissioned report on the state of the real estate industry.

Need I say more?

For those who don't have immediate access to this titillating document, chapter A1's subheading reads, "The real estate industry is saddled with a large number of part-time, untrained, unethical, and/or incompetent agents. This knowledge gap threatens the credibility of the industry."

Will I be slapped with an Article 15 violation for writing that? For repeating that statement about other real estate agents?

The DANGER Report was thoroughly researched and published by NAR. It can't be "false or misleading", can it? The conclusion reached above may in fact be one of the truest statements of all time. Article 15 only precludes repeating false and misleading statements. I'm repeating facts.

There's nothing unethical about stating what's true. I would encourage MORE people to share uncomfortable truths – to protect property sellers from abuse and ignorance.

The opening paragraph of Section A1's content states:

> The knowledge gap and competency gap from the most to the least is very large, due to the low barriers of entry, low continuing education requirements...to become a licensed

real estate agent requires an average of only 70 hours with the lowest requirement being 13 hours.

This chapter concludes, "And while this lack of agent knowledge is a significant danger in itself, when combined with a lack of basic competency it could be destructive and harmful both to the industry and the consumer."

Speak up. Demand more. Don't entrust your property sale to someone who lacks expertise and attentiveness.

At a minimum, go behind the scenes to review your potential agent's resume and work history. Look at their prior listings and check the quality of their past work. Call their previous clients to learn about whether the agent was helpful, responsive, and effective.

You won't secure the best investment if you hire someone who's working against you!

Real estate agents can and do lie and deceive property owners about the extent of their past clients' successes by omitting and manipulating numbers (See Chapter 7). They're prone to diverting attention away from the success of the CLIENT (aka Home Owner, aka Seller) to instead obsess over the success of the AGENT (aka themselves), often pitching their own numbers as though they will translate directly to your bank account - - - they won't!!

Bragging about themselves is a diversionary tactic to shift your focus away from yourself, your sale, your profit. To avert your attention away from the fact that they have no functional mechanism for pushing your profit to the next level, they put the focus on something they do know how to talk about – themselves – and they pretend that should be sufficient for you to trust them. They want more than anything to ride high on their brief, animated interaction with you and capitalize it into a signed listing contract before they leave your house. For your biggest asset. They want you to sign on without a clear game plan tailor-made for you. For your biggest asset?

Don't let your focus stray from *your* needs as you prepare to sell. The focus of *your* property sale should rightly be on *you*, *your* property, and *your* profit.

A skilled broker will enhance both your experience and your bottom line. Make sure that if you work with someone, they add literal value to your transaction – that they apply The Psychological Secrets That Sell Your Property for More.

Your Realtor should of course guard against basic listing errors (that doesn't sound like a lot to ask for, but it's mentioned here for a reason – basic errors are extremely prevalent). More than that, they should be a marketing professional who understands that every single detail about the listing must be designed to SELL the house. Not just to describe it. Not just to "list" it. But to SELL it. The listing presentation needs to come out swinging like a Shark Tank presenter, smiling broadly, connecting with the audience, knowing WHO we want to attract and specifically HOW we will attract them.

To achieve the highest prices, we ensure that clients get financially savvy, strategic advice on exactly where to invest in the property to attract the highest-paying buyer, and how to masterfully negotiate offers when we get them.

Don't let anyone tell you that there is one and only one price for your house. There are options in front of you when you're getting ready to go to market. These are very high-dollar decisions you're about to start making. Some of the most financially weighty decisions you may have made in your life. Make sure that the power is in *your* hands when you're making them.

Get a Psychological Selling expert on your side, who knows which strategies to implement in your case and how best to implement them to get you the highest return on investment for your property. Remember, as you're preparing your property, as you're interviewing agents, and as you list the home...

#1 Talk is Cheap. Seeing is Believing. - Show off those great property features so buyers can see why they should pay top-dollar.

#2 Know Your Product. Know Your Value. - The property's price must be right. Not low, not high, but just right. Pricing research must be done thoroughly, correctly, and in-depth to set the correct price.

#3 You Never Get a Second Chance to Make a First Impression – Buyers can't shake that initial gut instinct reaction to what they see first.

#4 Everybody Wants to Have What Everybody Else Wants to Have – If your property will make their friends jealous, they will eagerly offer top dollar to purchase it.

#5 Behind the Scenes - It's Where the Magic Happens - Every single thing about the property's marketing should be designed, written, and presented to SELL the property.

Psychology-based marketing produces results. Many considerations comprise this detail-oriented method. In concert, they have the appearance of working magic on the buyer. Once we turn on the magic, your life is easy. The hardest part becomes choosing *which* buyer to work with.

Lauren Collier

L auren Collier, Lauren@LiveDreamColorado.com, is a property consultant, marketing specialist, veteran real estate investor, Graduate REALTOR® Institute instructor, and Broker Owner of Live Dream Colorado (www.LiveDreamColorado.com), an aspirational, purpose-driven real estate firm dedicated to delivering expert advice, honest communication, best-in-class service, and community philanthropy. She has sold hundreds of properties and trained numerous REALTORS®. Lauren routinely engineers listing campaigns that exceed both clients' expectations and other real estate agents' predictions.

Lauren has earned a variety of professional awards and recognitions for her work including Peak Producer and Colorado 10 Best Real Estate Professionals for Client Satisfaction. She's a Master Certified Negotiation Expert, Designated Luxury Home Expert, Certified Military Relocation Professional, Military Housing Specialist, and Accredited Luxury Home Specialist. She holds a Bachelor's degree in biology (University of Colorado, Colorado Springs, magna cum laude, 2004) and a Master's degree in Elementary Education (University of Phoenix, 2007).

Lauren believes in giving back. As a champion for small business, Lauren hosts the Idea Accelerator Podcast, interviewing experts across all fields of interest to share their strategies for succeeding in business and beyond. As a local philanthropic leader, she has raised thousands of dollars for local schools and the nonprofit Trails and Open Space Coalition.

Lauren believes that property ownership is a meaningful personal experience for every person, bringing freedom, responsibility, stability, and comfort. Her passion is for helping property owners leverage their real estate investments to make their dreams come true.

Here is Lauren's story...

. . . . .

"Nope, this is not a love story...Well, not in the traditional sense."

At the time I thought with my $2000 in savings I was nearly rich.

My dog and all my wordly possessions packed into my Oldsmobile, I was driving 22 hours from Kentucky to Colorado. Twenty years old and a chronic overachiever in school, I had decided to take a break from college. I needed to do less studying and more living. Every minute of driving that long highway, I was looking forward to a simpler life, the good life in the Colorado mountains. Based on my experience working for a summer in Alaska, I assumed in Colorado Springs I'd quickly get a job for ten dollars an hour and an apartment for $400 a month, and I'd be all set.

WRONG. Colorado Springs economics were very different from Anchorage economics.

After a month-long job hunt, all I got was $5.15 an hour. My apartment rent was $600 per month. My budget was upside down from Day 1.

At the time I thought with my $2000 in savings I was nearly rich. Boy was I wrong. After security deposit and first month's rent, I was nearly broke already before I started. I didn't yet own a bed, table, microwave, a garbage can...

I was in a tough spot. I took a part-time second job, $5.75 an hour.

Even with two jobs, rent was crushing me. Always working and always exhausted, I had no money and no time. I felt very vulnerable and not in control. The simple life was not the good life for me! Then one day I met a man who changed my life.

Nope, this is not a love story...Well, not in the traditional sense.

That day I fell in love not with the person speaking, but with the words he said. The moments that day with a complete stranger changed my life forever.

I was downtown on a warm June day when a laid-back middle-aged guy in a Hawaiian shirt sitting on the Jose Muldoon's patio invited me to have a drink. I said I was only 20 so I couldn't drink. "Then we'll buy you a coke," he concluded.

"They" were an uncle, and his nephew "who didn't know how to talk to girls." That, I came to learn, was the reason the uncle had spoken to me. The nephew, sure enough, spoke maybe five sentences the whole time. But the uncle, I asked how he got so lucky to sit on the Jose Muldoon's patio in the middle of a weekday like this. Why didn't he have to go to work? "I haven't worked for years." he said.

"How'd you do that?!" I asked incredulously.

"I started investing in real estate when I was your age."

He talked about buying rental properties and making profit buying and selling real estate. He explained strategies of real estate investing, which today I understand, but at the time sounded like a foreign language. Here a guy who had learned to outsmart the system, so for many years now he's been able to travel the world and spend time with his family as much as he likes.

That sounded awesome to me!! He couldn't possibly have said anything more intriguing. Just a tiny bit of passive income – just a fraction of what he'd done – would stop this struggling and change my reality completely. That was the moment I became obsessed with real estate.

This was a total stranger - who opened the door to a new way of thinking. A minimum wage earner, I stewed constantly on how to increase my pay. But "never having to work again" was a revolutionary concept. What I saw growing up was my family working, all day, all night. That's "just what you do." My expectations changed forever in this moment. Collecting passive income, investing in appreciating assets, manipulating the system instead of the system controlling me – hearing these ideas was like being handed a secret treasure map.

The ideas got more urgent when he said "So have you bought a house?"

"No." (obviously) "I told you I'm only 20!" I replied incredulously.

Him: Do you pay rent?
Me: Yes.
Him: Does it go up every year?
Me: Yes.
Him: Do you like that?
Me: No.

"Then buy a house."

He bought his first property at my age – it set him apart from his peers and made his future possible. Owning your home was the cornerstone of his philosophy. When you're ready to move, you can turn it into a rental and make profit. Or, you can sell the house and get your equity back. At the very least, you get lots of tax savings every year for the mortgage interest payments. And if nothing else, you have a place to call your own, to fix and change the way you like.

This wasn't someone with anything to sell. He wasn't a real estate agent. He had no book or investing program to sell me. He was just an early retiree sharing with a younger person how to make a better life. Don't ask me what trajectory my life would have taken without that completely random encounter – I have no idea. But I do know for a fact that that day and that conversation changed the course of my life forever, and it set me on the track to who I am today.

There were bumps in the road between then and now - that's a story for another time. That day, my goal in life became to quit the rent cycle ASAP by buying a house and then get started in real estate investing.

·　·　·　·　·

"We aren't here to do things the easy way. We're here to do things the RIGHT way."

My dad was a Green Beret.

I didn't grow up thinking of us as a military family. Pop was no longer in the Army, so we didn't lead a military lifestyle as such. We didn't move. He barely talked about his military service.

But I did grow up with military values. Chief among them, the principle that we do not do things the easy way. EVER. We do things the RIGHT way. Always.

That's how it's done in the Collier household. From reading, writing, and arithmetic to toothbrushing, shoetieing, and video game playing. Yep, my dad was pretty obsessed with video games, and he'd MAKE me keep playing them until we won. If that meant staying up til 2am on a school night, unable to keep my eyes open, then so be it. That's the dedication level we're talking about. Absurd? Well sometimes, yes. But translate that to school work, test prep, and extracurricular activities – we didn't stop perfecting it until it was perfect. That was his way, and it became mine.

So you know when I shopped for my first house it had to be perfect.

I wanted to see everything before I made a decision. My agent was outgoing and friendly, but soon she had more important things to do. It seemed she wanted me to just hurry up and buy something. I was about to spend more money than I'd ever spent on anything – or than I thought I ever would spend on anything. And committing to a place to live for – so I thought - the rest of my life. That's SERIOUS business. No small decision! I didn't feel like my agent saw it that way.

First I missed out on the house I wanted to buy by acting too late. Then I put a Plan B property under contract and cancelled on inspection. Finally, I found another house nearby, wrote an offer, then cancelled even before inspection because I just wasn't happy. I was probably the worst client ever! But I just wanted the *perfect* house, and at the same time I felt rushed to move on *something*.

I finally selected a home – the one that reeked of cat pee – I'm telling you, you could smell it before you opened the door.

Perfect? Nope! But the price, size and location were perfect, so I compromised and decided to do the work myself.

The home buying experience left such a bad taste in my mouth that I quit fantasizing about real estate for a while after that. I moved on to other things...or tried to.

But I couldn't leave it alone. One day, some five years after buying that house, I finally looked in the mirror and admitted it to myself: "You are obsessed with real estate." It was and is my passion. I'm obsessed with the numbers, the value, the investment. But you know what else? I'm also completely, totally, 100% obsessed with service and satisfaction.

I don't ever, ever want anyone to have the buying process that I had.

My agents and I want each and every person, buyers and sellers, to have the type of process where you know we support you and your needs 100% of the time. You want the house? We want to help you buy it. You don't want the house? We want to help you see other ones. The only thing we don't want is for our clients to feel pressured, rushed, or stressed.

We are obsessed with the satisfaction and happiness of every single person we work with. And if we get too busy to help everyone, we'll hire another person who's service-obsessed too. We cannot have less. We do not want to be "just another agent" – pushy, in a rush, always having something more important to do.

Is it hard sometimes? Yep, sometimes it's hard. Do we stay up til 2am til our eyelids close and we can't work a minute longer – yep sometimes we sure do. Because we are passionate about our clients having a successful real estate experience.

Whether your dream house is easy or hard to find. Whether your property is easy or hard to sell. We want you to know that you can rely on us not to push and not to rush, but to support you in both a successful real estate transaction and a great overall experience.

We aren't here to do things the easy way. We're here to do things the right way... And then some.

· · · · ·

"I had NO real estate expertise at that time...But I'm no idiot."

A real estate investor ignited my passion for real estate. A bad real estate experience snuffed my dream of becoming a real estate agent. **Then came THIS crazy incident** - it kicked me into the business – after this I HAD to jump in.

When I needed to list my house many years ago, I interviewed several real estate agents. They all saw the inside of the house for the first time upon arrival. Yet they had all showed up with comps in hand and a predetermined sale price, selected before even viewing the home. They all made presentations about why they were right about the sale price they had made up before their visit.

Let me tell you a couple things about that house. It was on a busy street. It had no garage. It was very small. It wasn't particularly nice inside. The sale prices these agent brought with them? They were the sale prices of homes on quiet streets with a garage or carport. Why would my house sell for the same price as those obviously superior homes?

I had NO real estate expertise at this time. I hadn't done any independent research. **But I'm no idiot.**

I know that a house on a bust street with no garage doesn't sell for the same price as a house on a quiet street with a garage. Are these people crazy or just dumb? What worried me more than their factual errors, was that they were completely committed to their convictions. They were all 100% convinced that they could sell my home for an unreasonable figure.

This reoccurred for two days in a row with suit-and-ties sitting across the table from me, looking like they needed me more than I needed them.

Next evening came an agent who didn't have a glossy presentation binder. He didn't come in suit and tie - He wore khakis and a button-up shirt. He was older than middle age and had many years of real estate experience behind him.

He analyzed the home, the likely sale price, the costs of sale...And then he broke the news. My house was worth barely any more today than what I paid for it a year ago – and since I had rolled loan fees into my mortgage, and since there were costs associated with selling a house, it wouldn't be possible to sell this house without taking a loss.

Despite several other pairs of fancy-looking agents talking to me for quite some time about listing my house, everyone had failed to mention this reality – that if I sold now, my costs of sale would outweigh my equity, and I would have to pay to sell my house.

I knew this final agent was right. The house might sell for $5,000 more than what I bought it for the year before, but that wouldn't cover typical costs of sale. I had overlooked the fact that most real estate is a good investment - IF you hold it for a while. I learned my lesson through this experience for sure. If you know me, you know I often insist on learning things the hard way – through personal experience. I once heard a saying "It's too painful to learn everything by experience." I hadn't read that yet in my 20's ☺

Anyway, back to the listing of the house. I did not list it, and I later refinanced. But had I put it on market with any those first agents, it might still be sitting there today. They were completely convinced that my house had the same value as those others, even though my house's amenities were obviously - to anyone – inferior. Are you crazy? **I don't know, it just really upset me that people would come in my house. All dressed up. And lie to me.**

Maybe they were trained to inflate value at the presentation, and then do price reductions later. But if that's the case, they were in for a bad surprise. A price reduction would put me underwater, and I didn't have the cash to pay to sell. Maybe they were just truly not paying attention to what they were doing, which, I'm sorry but, when you're dealing with an asset as big as a house, is just inexcusable. That final agent spent an hour having a heartfelt conversation with me and didn't earn a dime for it, but I'm certain he sleeps well at night - knowing that he's honest with people and doesn't run a business built on deceit.

I'd truly prefer to think my experience was a fluke. But by now, having practiced real estate professionally for a while, enough people have shared with me their past real estate horror stories that I know this type of experience is common. Being misled, lied to, subjected to incompetence.

I have honed my practice to focus on sellers and their properties, providing in-depth research and analysis and accurate information. ...So I can provide the highest quality service to people who need it, which includes patient, honest conversations not just before going on market, but also while on market, during negotiations, and all the way until closing and beyond. ...So I can put in the time necessary to provide superior marketing, expert contract analysis, and well-thought-out recommendations. ...So I can provide not just accurate information, but also adequate time to each person's process, not just as clients but also as friends.

That's also why I wrote this book *The Psychological Secrets That Sell Your Property for More: How to make an extra $40,000* *of profit by thinking like a Shark Tank investor* - to help homeowners protect themselves when the time comes to sell their home. I hope this book will make a difference. (If you'd like to order a copy of the book for a friend, just complete the order form at www.giftlaurensbookforcharity.com and we'll rush a copy to you.)

Til Next Time,

Lauren

Lauren Collier

THE **MOST**
VALUABLE
Free Gift EVER

Learn How to Conserve Your Valuable Time and Avoid Uncertainty in your property sale – Initial Consultation Absolutely FREE

Including a FREE "Property Diagnosis" for the Fastest and Greatest Profit on your Property Sale

All You Have To Do is Go Here Now:
SellAHouseColoradoSprings.com

www.ingramcontent.com/pod-product-compliance
Lightning Source LLC
Chambersburg PA
CBHW071606200326
41519CB00021BB/6895